ENDORSEMENTS

This is fabulous!! I love the concept. I love the possibilities. If *Stretch Marks* can show me the way to happiness within myself, I'm coming along! And bringing the wine!!
Layne Rosen, Entrepreneur and Mother

Thoughtful, readable, practical. I loved it!
Jennifer Ellis, Ph.D., Epidemiologist and Mother

This book is an uplifting, feel-good, empowering, eye-opening read. Amber writes with her creative spirit and sense of humor in the driver's seat. The methods she describes not only help us find precious momentum towards our dreams but are both straightforward and inspiring.
Elysia Jordan, Actor and Godmother

Stretch Marks is a profoundly honest and brilliantly written guide for parents that will make you want to hug it tightly in your arms after reading and never, ever let go.
Angela Savoy, Artist and Mother

Every mother will love this book. And probably some Dads as well. I have been reading it with a big smile on my face, love her journey and insights. Entertaining and helpful, love her open approach. I honestly couldn't stop reading it!
Julie Hawksworth, CEO Micro Kickboard and Mother

I loved it. It has a lot of great tips that are, most importantly, easy to put into practice without a lot of time and stress.

Matthew Vlahakis, Math Specialist, Actor, and Father

This is great! I totally want to read more and follow Amber's program.

Tara Stern, Soccer Coach and Stay-at-Home Mother

I really LOVE the idea that pursuing your happiness is fruitful for all… and that it includes the happiness of your family. Because the planet is crawling with little people who, if we raise them right, will inhabit the earth and make it happier for everyone. Happiness begets happiness. I love it!!!!!

Jewels Washington, Stay-at-Home Mother

I love it! I found it to be a wonderful reminder of what is important.

Nate Chittick, Financial Analyst and Father

As a dad, I avoided the physical stretch marks of being a parent. But, I still suffer all the anxiety and uncertainty that one does. I didn't realize how much I needed this book until I started applying The Mindsets to my life as the parent of a five-year-old. The candid way Trueblood shares her own experience, coupled with a wide array of resource material and diverse references, makes *Stretch Marks* wholly relatable and informative to anyone committed to raising well-rounded children, while maintaining a healthy sense of self, service, and personal success. No book can tell you how to have it all, but *Stretch Marks* taught me how to have enough when I was in the trenches of parenthood, and how to aspire for more as the playing field levels out. It's more of a "You Can," than a "How To" book.

Jay Reto, Stay-at-Home Father

I have had this inkling of wanting to change my lifestyle for some time and Amber really inspired me to figure out how I can do that. I think this book is one the world could use.

Priscilla Sommer, CFO The Grand Bevy and Mother

Totally engages the reader right from the start!!

Gisa Nico, Director at Butterfly
Garden Preschool and Mother

Amber brilliantly and transparently walks you through her life as a mother of four and how she balances life on the road with love and gratitude. This is a must read for anyone looking to be happy in the mess of life and more purposeful in their relationships…especially the one with yourself.

Jeri Moran, Business Owner and Mother

I LOVE THIS!!!!…I want to read more!

Eve Stewart, Attorney and Mother

STRETCH MARKS

To Ann,
Be truly you!
♡ AMBER

STRETCH
MARKS

A Self-Development Tool for Mothers Who are Being Stretched in Every Direction

AMBER
TRUEBLOOD

NEW YORK

LONDON • NASHVILLE • MELBOURNE • VANCOUVER

STRETCH MARKS

A Self-Development Tool for Mothers Who are Being Stretched in Every Direction

Published in New York, New York, by Morgan James Publishing. Morgan James is a trademark of Morgan James, LLC. www.MorganJamesPublishing.com

ISBN 9781642794243 paperback
ISBN 9781642794250 eBook
Library of Congress Control Number: 2019900586

Cover Design by:
Megan Pearson, Jesse Wilson, Angela Savoy, and Jaimie Trueblood

Interior Design by:
Chris Treccani
www.3dogcreative.net

Arrow Drawing by:
Dylan Trueblood

Breathe Drawing by:
Cameron Trueblood

Morgan James is a proud partner of Habitat for Humanity Peninsula and Greater Williamsburg. Partners in building since 2006.

Get involved today! Visit
MorganJamesPublishing.com/giving-back

To my husband and my four boys,
You amaze me every day.

Special thanks to the many Children's Museums and Science Centers who educated, occupied, and inspired my children during our year-long U.S. adventure!

A portion of the proceeds from this book will support community outreach programs at the Science Centers and Children's Museums my family enjoyed while I sat in various hotels, coffeeshops, and airports writing *Stretch Marks*:

- Sausalito, California: Bay Area Discovery Museum
- Dayton, Ohio: Boonshoft Museum of Discovery
- Philadelphia, Pennsylvania: Franklin Institute
- Denver, Colorado: Children's Museum of Denver
- Detroit, Michigan: Michigan Science Center
- Dallas, Texas: Perot Museum
- Buffalo, New York: Explore and More Museum
- Phoenix, Arizona: Musical Instrument Museum
- San Francisco, California: Exploratorium
- Appleton, Wisconsin: Building for Kids Children's Museum
- Santa Ana, California: Discovery Cube
- Baltimore, Maryland: Maryland Science Center

- Philadelphia, Pennsylvania: Please Touch Museum
- New Orleans, Louisiana: Louisiana Children's Museum
- San Antonio, Texas: The DoSeum
- Kansas City, Missouri: Science City
- Madison, Wisconsin: The Children's Museum
- Grand Rapids, Michigan: Grand Rapids Children's Museum
- Schenectady, New York: miSci

TABLE OF CONTENTS

ACKNOWLEDGMENTS

My husband Jaimie completed 967 loads of laundry, washed 4,032 dishes, and managed our boys every day to give me the space, time, and silence I needed to write this book. He also kept them occupied with classic-rock jam sessions, which were not-so-quiet but too stinking cute to stop. This book would simply not exist without Jaimie's love, support, and superhuman ability to be both *fun* dad and *disciplinarian* dad.

My boys. I'm inspired by their kindness, their creativity, and their boundless energy. They're exhausting, very loud, and their feet stink to high heaven, but I wouldn't exchange them for anything in the world.

My dad taught me big dreams are always worth the effort. His consistent love and respect give me the confidence to always be myself and aim high. Although I did not inherit his cooking talent or his penmanship, he supported my dream to write this book and fully expects it will sell millions of copies. *But, no pressure.*

I'm so thankful to my mom for her 44 years of unending love, support, and friendship. Without her, I would not have inherited the *Sandahl Family Humor* (which is hilarious only to a small group of humans). She also taught me how to make fudge in a microwave, how to fix sprinklers, and has already convinced her book club to add *Stretch Marks* to their book list.

My sister Allison Reisz, (half-sister for those of you reading closely and questioning my *only child* status). I'm so grateful for her friendship, encouragement, millennial-related expertise, and ability to remind me as often as possible that I'm the *much* older sister.

Although many friends read and provided feedback as I wrote and rewrote *Stretch Marks*, I must give a very special thank you to Jay Reto, Jeri Moran, and Angela Savoy. Their ability to balance insightful critiques with kind compliments not only kept me writing but made this a better book. Much better.

A hundred years ago, Professor Richard Berg scribbled red ink all over my essay, placed a big "D" on my paper, and then taught me how to write. I cannot imagine how terrible this book would have been without his cutting honesty and his unique perspective on humanity. *Side story: a few years back I met my friend Delmy for lunch and recognized Dr. Berg seated outside. I was so flustered; I could not bring myself to approach him to tell him thank you. His influence on my writing and his ability to look at the world through multiple lenses made me a better writer and a better person.*

Dan Janal, my Developmental Editor, encouraged and guided me from the very beginning of my book proposal, through the entire manuscript, and even introduced my work to Terry Whalin at Morgan James Publishing. His kindness, expertise, and sage advice was essential. For example, Dan read a story from the middle of the book and said to me; *I think you have to lead with this story. I think it might even be your title.* Thank you, Dan, for *Stretch Marks*.

My copyeditor, Alison Cornford-Matheson showed never-ending patience and expertise as she fixed and massaged all my messy grammar problems and countless sentence fragments. *Countless* fragments. Alison removed hundreds of useless words such as 'that,' 'super,' 'very,' and 'really.' ~~That's what really made her so very super!~~ I mean, *Alison helped me maintain a real and relatable tone while improving the clarity, specificity, and strength of my words.*

I would like to thank Morgan James Publishing for believing in this first-time author and providing me with all the resources and support to make this book happen.

INTRODUCTION:

How to Read This Book

Are you exhausted?
Are you tired of putting everyone's needs and desires above your own?
Is someone calling, knocking at your door, or pulling on your arm as you try to read this page?
You are not alone.

You spent the last several years ensuring the people around you are alive and happy. You found their socks, made their special snacks, and got them to soccer practice on time. That takes *a lot* of time and energy.

Maybe it's been so long since you considered your own wants, you don't even know what they are anymore?

Think about it, what makes you happy and excited?
What makes you feel competent, confident, and content?

This book is in your hands because you're ready. It's time to uncover your dreams, unpack those forgotten talents, and discover what *you* want.

Every chapter will begin with a personal story (*so you'll know you're not alone in this journey*), provide lots of different tools and tricks (*because you have a unique personality, lifestyle, and set of values)* and highlight the Key Takeaways *(so you can easily remember the most important stuff)*. Many chapters also include a Mini-Homework Assignment. *Don't freak out!*

Here's an example Mini-Homework Assignment: The Three Minute Slow Down

The next time you take a shower, take an extra three minutes. Before you turn off the water and rush on to the next part of your day…Stop. If you forget and turn off the water before remembering today's Mini-Homework, then *turn the water back on.*

Spend three minutes or about 15 long, deep breaths, focused on something as simple and positive as possible. *Zone out.* Watch the water drip down the glass. Or, close your eyes and think of one simple thing you're grateful for. Or, imagine yourself happily alone in the mountains, desert, or on the beach. Three minutes to breathe and s l o w   d o w n.

It is extremely *unlikely* the world outside your bathroom door will spontaneously combust if you take these three minutes. It is *very likely,* however, you will enter the next part of your day happier and calmer. Whether you're on your way to a meeting, taking the kids to school, or finally turning into bed for the night, these three minutes can make a critical impact.

In Part I, you'll learn how to lessen the guilt and tune out the judgments and opinions of the world around you. You'll figure out which Mom Mode you're in, how to Focus Forward, and why life is easier when you flaunt your weaknesses.

Part II is all about parenting. You'll learn how to foster respect and kindness between your children and replace sibling *competition* with sibling *support.* You'll identify the Top Four traits you want to encourage in order to help you make better discipline decisions for your family. You'll determine family rules for devices and understand why it's helpful for your kids to know their parents are *not* perfect.

Delve into the A.M.B.E.R. Mindsets in Part III. This is the *meat* of the book. Salami, turkey, roast beef – all of it's in there. The Mindsets will show you how to figure out what you truly want (ASK), get going in the right direction (MOVE), stop the self-sabotage (BELIEFS), master your mind and body to feel happier and healthier (ELEVATE), and help the world by being *selfish* (RADIATE). I saved this section for Part III because if you're riddled with guilt or distracted by parental frustrations, it's much tougher to focus on your own needs, wants, and dreams.

In Part IV, you'll ease into visualization, meditation practices, and make your own Intention Bubbles. Whether you're skeptical, curious, or already an expert, you'll find tricks and techniques to make your journey smoother and faster.

While this book is written to read from start to finish, there are *no rules*. If you want to jump around, *do it*. If you want to skip the Mini-Homework Assignments, *no problem*. If you want to start at the end of each chapter, *go for it*. If you want to use this book as a coaster while you lounge in a hot tub and drink a martini, *I fully endorse it*!

Stretch Marks gives you the tools to:
- ✓ Create more time and space in your life.
- ✓ Reveal your natural interests and talents.
- ✓ Find the best tools according to your personality, lifestyle, and values.
- ✓ Inspire the changes that'll make you a healthier and happier parent, partner, friend, and human.

PS: I'd be honored if you scribble and circle and make notes all over this book. It means you're invested; you're fired up! Then, you can more easily find what tools you want to try and which tips you want to remember. Let's do this!

PART I

RELEASE YOUR BAGGAGE

Chapter One

SMASH YOUR *iSHOULDS*

All the Woulda-Coulda-Shouldas layin' in the sun,
talkin 'bout the things they woulda-coulda-shoulda done...
But those Woulda-Coulda-Shouldas all ran away and hid
from one little did.
Shel Silverstein

I have this one stretch mark that's longer and wider than all the rest. When I lie on my back, it looks like an earthworm crawled up on my stomach and died. A pet worm carcass, with me always.

Between all four of my pregnancies, I gained 178 pounds. For so long, I moaned and groaned about my belly rolls and how my thighs chafed against each other. *Vaseline helps a lot.* It was easy to overlook everything I put myself through, both emotionally and physically. Now, I'm grateful for all of it. That little worm is my badge of honor.

Do you remember when you became a parent? Do you remember when all of your own needs and wants and interests fell by the wayside? *I used to be so much smarter, funnier, thinner, and more interesting!* Parenting – it's the perfect storm of sleep deprivation, dirty laundry, and preparing the same boring meals a quadrillion times. Yes, parenting is amazing. But, it can also make you feel insane, or like a vampire bat attacked and drained all your mojo. You play the part of personal chef, private chauffeur, nursemaid, housekeeper, bookkeeper, toddler-stylist, financial manager, activities consultant, teacher, and baby-whisperer. Oh, and you often look like crap. *No offense.*

Do you fantasize about feeling a sense of accomplishment? Imagine if someone complimented you regularly. Dream about receiving acknowledgment for all your time and effort. *Ooh, this banquet is for me? What beautiful flowers! And a foot massage? How wonderful!*

The Bad News: *This will never happen in real life.*

The Good News: *You are not alone.*

I called this book *Stretch Marks* because those little worm carcasses represent so much more than the physical stretching of your skin. They are memory stamps of the major growth events in your life. Stretch marks are permanent, but not painful. You may have one or two, or maybe you're covered in them. Either way, you've endured an intense event. Your body accommodated.

It expanded, if you will.

Stretch marks aren't *only* physical. We have psychological and emotional stretch marks too. We all endure crises and go through significant changes in our lives, and we grow from these experiences. If every event was easy and painless, what would we learn? How would we change? Would we become better? Stronger? Wiser?

Can you remember a time when you saw a limit, a barrier, or a boundary, and you pushed through it? When have you persevered despite a huge setback? Maybe you experienced the death of someone you loved dearly. *How did that change you?* Maybe you lost a job, became seriously ill, or got divorced. *What did you learn?*

Think of the times you've pushed past your comfort zone and realized you're stronger than you thought you were. You're more powerful. More resilient. You have some stretch marks, my friend. Let's celebrate them.

A woman is like a tea bag, you never know how strong she is until she gets in hot water.
Eleanor Roosevelt

Crying in the Shower

The crap truly hit the fan when my youngest son, Evan, learned to walk. I felt like I'd been side swiped. I woke up disoriented and surprised to find myself with four sons, no career, two worthless master's degrees, and an intense feeling I had no individual identity. *Major first world problem, right?* I had been through a divorce, a bankruptcy, and an infertility diagnosis... but none of that hit me like being in the weeds with four small children.

The never-ending nature of parenting can make you curl into a ball on the shower floor and cry. You probably don't have the physical, emotional, and psychological support you so desperately crave. You go and go and go all day and all night. Then, someone comes along and shakes the Etch-A-Sketch that is your life, and you start all over again with absolutely nothing to show for all your hard work. *Not again?!*

Squash Your Bird

You probably listen to that little yellow bird. She's the bird of self-judgment. *You know the one?* She sits on your shoulder just waiting for the perfect moment to start chirping and chipping away at your confidence and self-worth. I can hear my little bird now. *You should be home more. You should be more patient. You should yell less. You should do some sit-ups.* When I hear her judgy chirps, I say, *Quiet, you! Fly away now, or I will squash you!*

What judgments does your little bird chirp about most often? What does your little bird say to you? Give her a name. Then, the next time you're fed up with her incessant chirping, just yell, *Shut your beak, Rebecca!*

Your *iShould* Devices

If you're not one for bird metaphors, you can try my high-tech version. Imagine your self-judgments as flashes and beeps and chirps from all of your devices. Your phone, tablet, and computer are harassing you from their various speakers and screens.

These, my friend, are your *iShoulds.*

iShould really go back to work now. iShould research elementary schools. iShould call the dishwasher repair company.

Please collect all of your *iShould* devices and put them on a big round table. Let them chirp away one last time. Then, grab the biggest mallet you can find in that awesome imaginative brain of yours and hoist it way up above your head. Now swing down hard with all your might and smash them up. See the tiny pieces flying across the room? Don't worry; you don't have to clean up *this* mess. If you're a self-proclaimed neat freak, just grab your imaginary garden hose and wash it all down the big drain in the center of the room.

The more you practice quieting your chirping bird or smashing up your *iShould* devices, the quicker you'll notice when they pipe up again. You become more aware. But, that's not all that happens. As you learn to ignore the distractions and silence those inner judgments, a clear picture will emerge.

Those clouds of self-doubt dissipate and what you want in your life shines through.

Unfortunately, you're so accustomed to running full speed ahead, whisked along in the rushing current of your life. You might surface for a breath now and then, panting and frantic. But, let me ask you this, who's driving your boat? You? Your boss? The kids? Who knows where this river leads? What if your actual destination is somewhere different? What if you're doing all this work only to end up in a place that will ultimately leave you unhappy? Maybe it's time you took the wheel, or the rudder – *whatever steers a boat.*

What will make you feel calmer? More satisfied? Happier? The tools and stories in this book will help you blow away those dark, stormy clouds so you can once again see clearly. You can find a future that is perfect for *you.* Not perfect for your mother-in-law. Not perfect for your boss or your neighbor. But, perfect for *you.* Stick with me, and you'll leave behind the guilt and the *iShoulds* to captain your own ship without the influence of the outside world.

Smash your iShoulds.

Your Top Five

You only have so many hours in a day, only so much energy. It's critical to stop and think: *How do I want to spend my precious time and limited resources?* Think back to yesterday. What did you spend most of your time doing? How did you spend your mental and emotional energy? Now ask yourself, *did those thoughts and actions line up with what's most important to me?* If not, then this is a great place to start.

Let's get clear on what is most important to *you,* at this point in your life.

Quick Quiz: MY TOP FIVE

Check off the FIVE areas that are most important to you at this particular time in your life:

- [ ] **Spending Time with Friends**
- [ ] **Playing Music/Listening to Music**
- [ ] **Problem Solving**
- [ ] **Being in Nature**
- [ ] **Feeling a Sense of Accomplishment**
- [ ] **Spending Time with Family**
- [ ] **Exercise (Specifically: _____)**
- [ ] **Cooking**
- [ ] **Traveling**
- [ ] **Helping Others**
- [ ] **Writing**
- [ ] **Reading**
- [ ] **Inspiring Others**
- [ ] **Making Art**
- [ ] **Spending Time Alone**
- [ ] _____
- [ ] _____
- [ ] _____

Put another way, which FIVE would you be devastated if you could never do again? What if you experienced each of your TOP FIVE every single day? Would you feel fulfilled, happy, and excited about your life? If not, go back and look again. Or, write in whatever I missed. I won't take offense. This is about *you. Remember that.*

You know *you*.

Don't worry; I know you still need time and energy to attack the mountain of chores necessary to keep your household and family afloat. **This guidebook is about managing all the mundane while still learning to live the life that is perfect for *you*.**

My Story: Clearing the Clouds

I thought I might lose my mind. I lost sight of what was important to me. I needed help. I remember pulling my car over, and sitting against a tree by myself, just a mile from home. It was one of those giant birch trees with a straight, white trunk, and bark that peels off like big paper scrolls. I sat there crying, wondering why I couldn't bring myself to drive home.

The next morning, I set up an appointment with a life-coach named Victoria. She was the mom of a good friend and offered to give me a free session. I felt lost. Busy, but incredibly bored. Massively thankful, but terribly frustrated. I was all set with my journal, some books, a pen, and my many lists. I walked into her office, sat down, and built up my little protective barrier of books and papers. Victoria looked at me and said, "Oh, you won't be needing any of that. By the way, are you a crier?" I looked at her, and my stomach dropped. "Yeah, I'm a crier." She nodded to a nearby tissue box, and I grabbed hold of it.

This wasn't going to be quite what I'd expected. She sat, took a breath and slowly asked, "So, Amber, what... do... YOU... want?" I don't remember ever feeling so vulnerable or so exposed. I twisted in my seat. No lists or books were going to save me.

What *did* I want?

I thought about it. My mind buzzed with a million chirping birds. *Did I pay the gardener? Are the property taxes due again already? Christopher needs a dentist appointment. Oh, and Michael's new school sent over all those forms.*

Another minute passed. My eyes slowly welled up with tears. "Peace," I answered.

With four boys under the age of seven at the time, you're probably not surprised to hear my answer. For me, it was a revelation. *Sometimes, we're the last to know.*

Victoria's next question was even more piercing. "Amber, when was the last time you made a decision from your heart?" I couldn't even process the question at first. *Huh?* I had to clarify, "You mean, a totally *irrational* decision?"

"Ouch," she said. My snotty attitude about emotionally-based decisions was clear. I fell quiet and thought about her question. A few more minutes passed. Then, it rushed to the surface. "When I decided I wanted a third child. And, again when I wanted a fourth." Those were literally the ONLY instances I could remember. I allowed my heart to make a big life decision only twice.

Was I happy with those choices? *Definitely.*

Were they totally logical and rational decisions? *Definitely not.*

At that moment, I realized how much I'd been ignoring my emotional side. I needed to learn to listen to my gut again. It wasn't easy. It took me two years from that day to learn how to balance my head with my heart. But, that meeting with Victoria was a turning point for me. That's when I stopped looking outside myself for happiness and started asking myself some very real questions. Most importantly, I realized only *I* could answer those questions.

Here's what my heart wanted: I wanted more peace. I wanted less responsibility for the tedious tasks of motherhood. I wanted more time enjoying my children and less time *managing* them. I wanted to challenge my brain. I wanted to do *more* than buy groceries, pay bills, organize activities, and schedule appointments. I wanted to travel to warm, beautiful places.

I also realized my priorities didn't match up with how I spent my time and my energy. I was so busy trying not to drown in the torrential current of my life, I didn't have a moment to stop and look around. I was too exhausted to decide what I wanted next. *Sound familiar?*

When one door of happiness closes, another opens;
but often we look so long at the closed door that we
do not see the one which has been opened for us.
Helen Keller

Frustrated?

What happens when you spend your time, money, and energy in a way that doesn't match up with your dreams and values? Yep. Frustration. Maybe your bank account is a disaster, but your career is confidently on track? Or, you're great at prioritizing your physical health, but your romantic relationship is a hot mess? How is it possible to have success or happiness in one area of your life, but feel you're drowning in another?

Well, it happens all the time.

In the next section, I'll share the framework that helped me break through those clouds of frustration. I matched my time and efforts with my TOP FIVE priorities. The fog of guilt dissipated. I'll show you the tools and tricks I used to figure out what I wanted. Then, I'll spell out a slew of tools to help you make it happen. Next, we'll move on to uncover any sabotaging beliefs.

Just a couple of years ago I felt overwhelmed, bored, tired, resentful, and guilty. Now I'm traveling across the U.S. with my family for a year. My two eldest sons are cast members in the U.S. touring company of the Broadway musical, *School of Rock*. We've visited 32 cities in the past eleven months and have another 17 cities ahead of us. I also have a contract to publish my first book and just spent a week in Costa Rica on a writers' retreat. Yes, I'm often still exhausted. But, it's a happy exhaustion. Instead of looking forward to the next time I can crawl back into bed, I'm excited for tomorrow.

Framework: The Five Mindsets

Here's the framework. I've split it into Five Mindsets: Ask, Move, Believe, Elevate, and Radiate. Yep, you guessed it, The A.M.B.E.R. Mindsets. *I thought I'd make it easy to remember.* The A.M.B.E.R. Mindsets are a roadmap to help you figure out what you want and what might be stopping you from achieving it. I'll lay out lots of tools for you to choose from, depending on your lifestyle, personality, and goals. Not only will you be happier, but I guarantee those around you will benefit too. *Feel free to send me some chocolate as a thank you.*

 **You cannot get what you want unless you know what it is, think it is possible, and believe you deserve it.**

Mindset "A" is for ASK

Ask yourself, *What Do I Want?* This is the first step. No amount of skills, information, time, or resources will help if you do not know *what* you want. Sometimes, it's not so simple to figure out. When you've spent several years focused on children, taking care of aging parents, or working in a career you hate, it's easy to forget what you enjoy. Or, maybe you think it's too late? Or, you believe it's too selfish to pursue it? You'll use fun tools like The Eulogy, Wear A Cowboy Hat, Pick Two, and The Opposite Game to find clarity about what *you* truly want.

Mindset "M" is for Move

In this mindset, you already know what you want. *Not for the REST of your life, just right now at this point in time.* Now it's time to get moving and make it happen. *But, how?* In the MOVE Mindset, you'll consider your personality, your TOP FIVE, and your lifestyle. Then, you'll lay out the best plan of action *for you.* You'll learn tricks like how to Be A Duck, Make More Time, Stop It, and Gamify It, to get you moving forward in a new direction.

Mindset "B" is for Believe

Once you know what you want and you're using the tools and skills to access it, you'll dig into your subconscious. What beliefs are stopping you or slowing you down? You'll use tools like The Baloney Beliefs Quiz and The Poop Mole Challenge to help you uncover and then smash the unhelpful beliefs floating around in your mind.

Mindset "E" is for Elevate

Now, it's time to ELEVATE. Here, you'll take the goals from the ASK Mindset, the tools from the MOVE Mindset, and the new healthier beliefs from the BELIEVE Mindset, and pull everything together. You'll learn how certain chemicals and hormones related to stress and anxiety can influence your blood pressure, metabolism, quality of sleep, and emotional reactivity. *Want to feel calmer? Sleep better? Quiet the chaotic chatter in your head?* In this Mindset, you'll learn hacks for your body (breathe, chew, eat, and move) and your mind (Let It Be, Forgiveness, and Gratitude) to elevate your life to another level.

Mindset "R" is for Radiate

In the RADIATE Mindset, you'll determine how you can use everything you've learned so far and RADIATE it outward.

You'll learn how helping others can benefit you both physically and psychologically. It's selfishly good. Focus your time, resources, and energy on a group or a cause beyond yourself, so you can be a happier, healthier role model and an inspiration to colleagues and friends.

A Quick Review: The FIVE Mindsets

(Because seriously, who can remember all of that?)
The ASK Mindset: Figure out what you want.
The MOVE Mindset: Choose tools you will use.
The BELIEVE Mindset: Uncover self-sabotaging beliefs.
The ELEVATE Mindset: Learn how to sleep better, feel calmer, and improve your mood.
The RADIATE Mindset: Use what you've learned to help a cause that's important to you.

MINI-HOMEWORK ASSIGNMENT (90 Seconds)

1. Name your bird:_____
   (Default name: "Paprika")
2. Write out your TOP FIVE. Use the notes page in your phone, post them on your computer, or write them out in bright red lipstick on your bathroom mirror.
   ✓ For Example: *I want to be with my family, dance, help others, travel, and learn something new.*

You cannot always control who walks into your life. But, you can control which window you throw them out of...
Anonymous

Chapter Two

KINTSUGI YOURSELF

We can all dance, if we find music that we love.
***Giraffes Can't Dance** by Giles Andreae*

Although my talk with Life-Coach Victoria led to a huge realization, I didn't know what to do next. How was I supposed to begin when all I could hear were my *iShoulds*? *iShould be so happy! iShould be so grateful! iShould chill out and realize my children are still young.* There will be plenty of time for me and my needs, later. Right?

Everyone I complained to told me to relax and enjoy this time...*blah, blah, blah.* I couldn't relate and could not take their advice. Not only was it unhelpful, but it also made me feel terrible. Why couldn't I enjoy and be grateful for everything I already had in my life? *What was wrong with me?*

My Story: The Hip-Hop Solution

The trickle of an answer seeped in when my two oldest sons attended a hip-hop dance class. I watched them through the glass and recorded every moment on my phone. Later that night, I noticed something that would forever change my life.

In the video, I could see my reflection in the glass. I had the biggest smile plastered across my face. I looked so silly. But, it made me realize how long it'd been since I had smiled like that. I needed to find that smile again.

I still heard Rebecca's incessant chirping: *You can't start dancing at 40! You don't have time to drive all the way to Hollywood for a class! You can't dance with kids half your age! You look ridiculous!* But here's the funny thing: If one of my children fell in love with dancing, would I drive to Hollywood? Would I find the time? Would I make it a priority?

You bet I would.

So, I drove to Hollywood twice a week to attend a dance class at the top studio in Los Angeles. After a few weeks, Rebecca quieted. Instead, a cute little monkey even showed up to give me high fives after class! *Monkeys can be supportive and enthusiastic like that.* I call him Marco. Now, when I have a *gut* feeling about something, I think of my *Monkey Gut*. And, I try to listen to it. Soon, it didn't matter that some of the other dancers were three decades younger than me or I that was the only one dressed for a yoga class. Once I let go of all my self-judgment, I had a blast!

It turns out, i*Should* dance.

If you hear a voice within you say 'you cannot paint,' then by all means paint and that voice will be silenced.
Vincent Van Gogh

I hated doing dishes. I complained about making chicken with rice and broccoli for the millionth time. But, once I invested more time in activities that brought me joy, my other responsibilities weren't nearly as irritating. Yes, I still had to do it all. But, it didn't drive me nuts like before. Adding enjoyable tasks to my days made me feel less bored, less resentful, and much happier.

Those daily annoyances that had irritated me SO MUCH went from giant boulders to tiny pebbles I barely noticed. Before this, I felt so *busy*. I never imagined *adding* to my to-do list was the answer.

What *happy-tasks* could you add to your daily workload, if it meant less resentment and more contentment in your life? Seriously, stop to think of a few.

For Example: call an old friend. Go for a walk around the block. Take 30 minutes to do a puzzle with a cup of tea. Sit while you eat dinner and don't get up for anything. Take a nap. Hide in your closet and watch an episode of *The Office* while you're supposed to be in the shower. Skip the PTA meeting and go to a movie alone. Watch an online lecture about something you find interesting. Grab a giant bag and fill it up with items you no longer use, then drive it over to a donation center. Get back into a hobby you abandoned years ago or make plans with a friend you haven't seen in far too long.

You Are *Not* Perfect

Sometimes your happiest place is where you least expect it. I never thought I would be a stay-at-home mom. I never thought I would have FOUR children. I never thought I would homeschool those children. I never thought my skateboarding, book-obsessed sons would end up in an Andrew Lloyd Webber musical.

If you told me twenty years ago that's where I'd be, on a 16-month U.S. tour with my entire family, I'd have laughed aloud and said, "Clearly you have me confused with someone else!" Actually, if you told me a year ago that's where I'd be, I flat out wouldn't have believed you.

You're on your own and you know what you know.
And you are the one who'll decide where to go.
Dr. Seuss

Before we move on to details and action steps, I want to give you a warning. It's very easy to get wrapped up in self-blame. Guilt. Even shame. You spend so much time beating yourself up; you have no energy left to move forward. You may even have a mental list, a running tally of things you could be doing better or things you think you're doing wrong.

No, you are *not* perfect. That is OK. Actually, not *only* is it OK, it's great! If you *were* perfect, how would you ever learn? How would you grow? What crazy stories would you have to tell your niece or your neighbors? Your mistakes, your inadequacies, and your wacky history make you unique and interesting. I recommend you make lots of mistakes. Then, be grateful for each one. You are not a perfect partner. You are not a perfect employee. You don't look perfect, smell perfect, or act perfectly. Me neither. *Cheers! We're not perfect!*

Kintsugi Yourself

In Japan, there's an art form called Kintsugi. An artist uses lacquer mixed with gold powder to fill cracks or breaks in a vase. The golden veins render the pottery more valuable. In this art form, damage is an important part of an object's history. Flaws are accentuated, not hidden.

Seriously, don't just skim past this. Stop and ponder it for a moment. Unless you're in a morgue, you've survived something difficult, and it's crucial to give yourself credit for that. What do you know now that you didn't before? Like Kintsugi, you've increased your value as a result of that experience. Maybe you learned something about others or yourself? Maybe you now have a hilarious story to tell? Maybe you became more resilient and confident knowing what you're capable of surviving?

You can try to hide your flaws and weaknesses. You can feel embarrassed and self-conscious. You can spend a ton of time focusing on your faults or complaining about them to your friends, or you can *Kintsugi* yourself! Highlighting your faults instead of hiding them will help you relax and become more likable and relatable.

Increase your value and your likeability by flaunting your flaws.

How Do I Kintsugi Myself?

If you're about to walk into a meeting feeling disorganized and flustered, step in and say, "Wow, I'm a total wreck this morning and feel like my brain hasn't even switched on. I'm so sorry. If you'll give me a minute, I'll pull myself together, and we can get started." Make it clear you're not trying to fool anyone, including yourself. This is a powerful tool.

Women are never stronger than when they arm themselves with their weaknesses.
Madame Marie du Deffand

Successful entrepreneurs and salespeople use this tactic brilliantly. Many folks think it's their job to figure out how you are lacking, lying, or just plain wrong. Pointing out your faults up front can put your audience at ease and allow them to truly listen. Being honest and open about your weaknesses breaks down our natural defensiveness. *Oh, you're not perfect? Great! Me neither!*

Nobody likes someone who acts like they're *perfect*. Try it out. I think you'll find it SUPER freeing and extremely effective.

Warning!! If you're someone who has *no problem* focusing on your weaknesses, this is **not** a free pass to go on and on *and on* about them.

Do you talk about your flaws all the time? Do you point them out to your Uber driver or discuss them at length with the mailman? This is not what I'm recommending. No. Call yourself out on the weakness, then move on to the good stuff. Spend most of your energy focusing on what you enjoy doing and what you excel at. Focus on your strengths and talents.

Are you incredible with people and enjoy speaking and leading large groups? Great! So, should you spend a lot of time improving your writing skills? What about your organizational skills?  Bookkeeping? Don't waste time and energy working on your weaknesses UNLESS one of those weaknesses specifically blocks you from maximizing your strengths.

Focus on your strengths, accept your weaknesses, and work on improving them *only* when they limit you.

Focus Forward

Do you focus on your past with regret, anger, or anxiety? *Why did I do that?* Do you replay yesterday's conversations over and over in your head? *I'm such an idiot!* Do you relive events in your mind that were stressful, sad, or irritating? *What is wrong with me?*

It's totally normal. But, while you're busy angrily or regretfully obsessing about the past, the planet is moving forward. It's progressing. Your life is not an episode of The Twilight Zone or Black Mirror (even though it may feel that way at times). Everyone else is *not* suspended in space, indefinitely waiting for you to pull yourself together. Nope. Time moves forward.

I look to the future because that's where I'm going to spend the rest of my life.
George Burns

Let me ask you this: what if the planet *could* pause and wait while you gripe and moan about past mistakes? What if we all could wait long enough for you to obsess about all the wrongs you've suffered? How long would you need for that? A couple hours? A few months? A decade?

Instead, what if you acknowledge your weaknesses? Acknowledge your losses, your imperfections, and your grief. *Briefly.* Then, move on. Face forward. Look to where you want to go next. What if you focus on what you enjoy? Focus on what makes you smile? If you don't know what that is, it's likely because you've spent far too long absorbed in your weaknesses or past screw-ups. Time moves forward. If you're perpetually focused on the past, you're missing out on the present. More importantly, you're preventing yourself the opportunity to captain your own ship.

Purpose Pockets

A great way to get out of this rut is by using *Purpose Pockets.* As you go through your day, pause for a few seconds before each *pocket.* A pocket could be a meeting at work, soccer practice with the kids, or dinner out with your new clients. Immediately before each pocket, take a few seconds and decide what you want. For example: *Tonight, I want to have a delicious dinner with my family and get reconnected, with no devices and lots of smiles and laughter.* It's simple and shouldn't take a lot of thought or preparation. Go with *your Monkey Gut* on this one.

Purpose Pockets force you to make conscious choices throughout your day. These choices are then more likely to align with what is *truly* important to you. Your focus shifts from what you *do not want* in your life to what you *do want* in your life.

Benefits of Purpose Pockets
- Allows you to focus on the present
- Puts you back in the captain's seat
- Reminds you what is most important

How To Do It:
Choose 2-3 things you want to do, on *purpose*, during the next *pocket* of your day.
- You can keep a little notebook
- You can say it or just think it
- You could sing it in your car

MINI-HOMEWORK ASSIGNMENT (3 minutes)

1. What weaknesses or faults will you Kintsugi?
2. Name one awful experience that made you smarter, stronger, or more resilient.

Imperfection is beauty, madness is genius, and it's better to be absolutely ridiculous than absolutely boring.
Marilyn Monroe

Chapter Three

LISTEN TO YOUR *MONKEY GUT*

You're mad, bonkers, completely off your head.
But I'll tell you a secret. All the best people are.
Alice in Wonderland by Lewis Carroll

Have you ever shopped alone at Target, calm and relaxed, responsible only for yourself for an entire 90 minutes? Then, you walk past one of those mirrored columns next to the shoe department and barely recognize the hot mess in the mirror – no makeup, a threadbare scrunchy, and deodorant stripe down your shirt. *Did I leave the house looking like this? At least I brushed my teeth. Or did I?*

All day you climb *up* a down escalator. When you stop to rest for a moment, you find yourself back at the bottom, starting over with even more laundry, bills, and emails in your inbox. So, how do you escape this sadistic down escalator of life?

That's why you're here my friend. Let's figure it out.

I've filled this book with the tricks and tools that took me from crying in my shower to writing my first book and feeling happier and more fulfilled than ever. You'll want to consider your unique situation, your values, and your personality. Once you figure out what you want most in your life, you will use the tools and tactics most likely to work for *you*.

You are not alone.

It will get better.

You're already doing a fantastic job!

My Story: A Traveling Troupe of Truebloods

You might ask, *how the heck do you travel with four children to 34 cities in a year? Do you ride in a tour bus? Do you stay in hotels? Why would you do this?*

Here's how it goes: We stay in rental houses and fly almost everywhere because there's not enough time in between shows to drive to the next city. Plus, I might strangle someone if I had to sit in a car with all my children for hours and hours every week. Since we don't stay in the company hotels, I make our own bookings and schedule our transportation for each city.

I've officially worked on this chapter in Denver, Las Vegas, San Francisco, Dallas and now Madison, Wisconsin. Each week on the road involves homeschooling, researching rental houses, finding flights, and booking rental cars. Plural. *Two* cars. (I haven't yet figured out how to fit every*thing* and every*one* into one car.) Each Sunday, we pack up two guitars, a bass, a keyboard, a drum set, five scooters, six skateboards, pads and helmets, clothes, and tons of books. *Southwest Airlines, please let me know if you find the ukulele we left in Denver!*

On Mondays, we all hop on a plane and move to a new city where we order groceries, do laundry, and unpack. It never fails;

I end up repacking several bags while sitting on a questionable carpet at the airline check-in desk. Curse that 50lbs. limit! Trying to find things on Monday nights is an infuriating treasure hunt.

During the week, we take our brood to museums, Skype with tutors, take over skateparks, and explore the city. I've scraped ice from windshields in Buffalo, cleaned up bloody noses in Tempe, and had a head-cold in Minneapolis that left me bedridden for two days.

No, I'm not a super-mom. Nor am I insane. This is the life that's right for *me*, right now. My point here is nobody else's life is right for *you*. A few years ago, this same experience would have been my biggest nightmare. Now, I'm spending my time and my energy and my money on my Top Five: Family, Education, Travel, Health, and Writing. It's awesome.

Who Are *You*?

What type of lifestyle energizes you? What sort of people leave you feeling content, safe, and happy? Maybe you don't know what your ideal situation is right now. Keep in mind one person's fantasy is another's nightmare and what sounds like a nightmare now may seem dreamy a few years down the line.

There are two great days in a person's life – the day we are born and the day we discover why.
William Barclay

The Mom Modes

Before we dig deeper, let's get clear on something: do you know what kind of 'help' you need most right now? Life changes drastically from one year to the next. Even a year can make a huge difference in what you have the time and energy to pursue. All the advice and tips and tools in the world won't help you if you're not sure what you need.

Is 90 minutes alone in Target your idea of paradise? If so, you might be in the mode I call **Sleepy in Sweatpants**. You know you're here when running errands alone is the highlight of your week. Or, maybe you only dream of such luxury? You are *in the weeds*. The main problems here are social isolation *(remember date nights?)*, unmet physiological needs *(remember sleep, exercise, and good food?)*, and insufficient emotional support *(someone hug me without wiping their nose on my shirt please!)*.

In **Sweatpants** mode, you consider a day without crying, yelling, or eating an entire tray of brownies *winning*. It makes total sense. If you're a parent and you don't put your baby's needs before your own for the first several months of their lives, they may not survive. The trick is this: Figuring out when it's healthy to move that *percentage of sacrifice* from 100% to 90% to 80% to 70% and so on.

If you're in **Sleepy in Sweatpants** mode, you may need to:

1. Get More Sleep. Instead of spending 20 minutes before bed on your phone, TV, or computer, turn it off. Say three things you're thankful for, then close your eyes. *Don't even read this book!* Just breathe and notice your thoughts. Try not to get wrapped up in them. The meditation chapter at the end of this book will show you how to start a practice that feels right for you. In the meantime, get ahold of a sound machine, blackout curtains, and have the kids draw a no-entry sign for your bedroom door.

I studied, met with medical doctors, scientists, and I'm here to tell you that the way to a more productive, more inspired, more joyful life is: Getting enough sleep.
Arianna Huffington

2. Spend Time with Adult Women – in person is best. Get a neighbor to go on a quick walk with you. Make friends at the park, market, or anywhere. Believe me; those other moms are just as desperate for a social connection. These people need not become life long friends, so don't worry about being super picky. My doula (basically an Olympic coach for women in labor) recommends 20 minutes minimum, per day with other adult females. Since I work from home and live with five *males*, this is something I have to pursue consciously. *While it doesn't always happen, if I'm grouchy, at least I know why.*

Note: Beware of Vampires! I know I said not to be picky, but you must avoid vampires. These blood suckers are people who zap your energy. They leave you feeling exhausted and drained. Notice how you feel after spending time with someone. Do you feel calm, happy, and excited? Or, do you feel irritated and mildly depressed? Say NO to vampires. *You need all the energy you can get.* If you live or work with one, this is tricky, and I'm sending you a big virtual hug right now.

3. Get A Hug. Ask a loved one for a 7-second hug once a day. Most women need daily, physical, non-romantic touch. *And no, your 4-year-old dragging himself along the floor attached to your leg does not count!*

4. Get Words of Appreciation. The secret to this one is a bit counter intuitive but try it anyway. *Give* genuine words of appreciation. Not to just anyone. Give these words to

the same folks you want to hear appreciation from most. The key is this: you have to do it genuinely and with no expectation of return. *Make it a game.* See if you can do it three times a day for three days. Then, give yourself a nice big, guilt-free treat when you're done. Even if you're feeling irritated and resentful toward everyone, try to find *something* to compliment. If done genuinely and consistently, you will see magical results.

Bed, Bath & Beyond Bored

Maybe your job is less demanding now or your children are in school or daycare? You're getting more sleep. You had time to blow-dry your hair last week. But, you still haven't been able to put yourself first in any truly meaningful way. You still spend most of your time and energy on the survival or advancement of others. You can't seem to remember what you're good at, what you used to do with your time, or how to move on to the next phase of your life.

You know you're in this mode when you're finally getting sleep, and you've got a handle on the kids or work, but you're *so bored.* Every day you're busy with thoughtless, tedious, never-ending tasks. Yet, nothing ever feels *done.* There's no sense of accomplishment. You'd love to add something new into your life but feel there's no time or space for anything else.

If you're in the **Bed, Bath and Beyond Bored** mode, you may need to:

1. Remember what makes you happy. Do it in small chunks. *Take a walk, read something funny, exercise, or call a friend you miss.*
2. Feel like you're accomplishing something. No, not just paying bills, buying groceries, and getting to your dentist

appointment once a year. *Give yourself a new task, do it, then celebrate it!*

3. Delegate the stuff you dislike doing. Teach the kids to do it, trade chores with your partner, or leave it undone for the day. *Teach your nine-year-old to do the laundry, load the dishwasher, or put away the groceries.*

Search & Rescue

You're in the **Search & Rescue** mode when you're so fed up, you're actively looking for a change. You're up late joining internet groups, listening to new podcasts, or checking out the self-help aisle at the local Barnes & Noble. You're ready to do whatever it takes to bring something new into your life.

If you're in the **Search & Rescue** mode, you may need to:

1. Decide. Don't just wish or daydream. *Decide.* The world is filled with people who wish for their lives to change. You have to *decide* it will change. It's a mental game. But, it makes a big difference.

2. Set MicroGoals. Make the goal so incredibly tiny, it'd be embarrassing *not* to do it. Do it at the right time for *you:* before you check your Instagram, right after the kids leave for school, or while you're on hold for a conference call. Then, you can reward yourself afterward with a muffin and a latte. *Unless your MicroGoal is reducing your caffeine or gluten intake.*

Do you listen to your intuition? If you are like me, you've ignored your instincts for so long, they've become stone quiet. It's so loud and chaotic in my house. It's hard to focus or slow down enough to think. When you *do* slow down, all you want is 30 minutes of mind-numbing Netflix or a big glass of wine and a cozy bed. *Right?* Then, as soon as that's over, you're bombarded with your *iShoulds*. You're pestered by that chirping bird. But now, it's time for Rebecca to fly away and bother somebody else. Marco the Monkey will be your new animal guide. Marco has *your* happiness in mind. That little monkey will give you a nudge in the right direction. You just have to listen closely.

Can you hear your Monkey Gut? He might be shy after years of being ignored. Luckily, the more you pay attention, the louder he'll become.

Listen to your *Monkey Gut*.

What makes others happy won't necessarily make you happy, and vice versa. Listen to Marco. He represents your internal compass, always pointing toward happiness. Allow yourself to let go of what the outside world thinks you should do with your time and energy, and you'll find yourself making smarter decisions about your life and your future.

Easier said than done, right? Well, that's why you're here my friend. It's a process. You will learn to smash your *iShoulds*, shoo away Rebecca and tune in to Marco. By the end of this journey, you'll feel inspired, motivated, supported, and confident in yourself and your decisions.

Let's do this.

Seize the moment. Remember all those women on the Titanic who waved off the dessert cart.
Erma Bombeck

PART II

LIFE WITH CHILDREN

Chapter Four

THE LIFE-LABORATORY

Promise me you'll remember you are
braver than you believe, stronger than you seem,
and smarter than you think.
Winnie-the-Pooh by A.A. Milne

When my son Christopher was three years old, Danny was 18 months, and I was seven months pregnant with Michael, we spent the summer living in Georgia. My husband, Jaimie, worked as the stills photographer on the movie *Fast Five,* filming in Atlanta. In those days, we traveled together wherever Jaimie's work took us: Cleveland, New Orleans, San Francisco, Puerto Rico, and eventually Oahu.

One night, a wave of guilt hit me. I realized I had a habit of saying sweet things to Christopher just after he fell asleep each night. But, I never did this with Danny. Rebecca piped up, *You're a terrible parent!*

For a peek into my crazy little brain, any guess what I would say to my oldest? *You will have a photographic memory.* Weird, I know. Anyway, that night I crept into the little bedroom where Danny slept in a borrowed Pack 'n Play, put my hand gently on his back, and spoke softly. *Mommy loves you so much and...* Immediately, Danny's eyes popped open, and he burst into tears.

Apparently, I knew on some level *not* to try my bedtime routine with this little guy. Instead of trying to make everything fair, I should have listened to my *Monkey Gut*.

Danny's the one who ended up with the photographic memory, so go figure.

Selfish Parenting

As a parent, I try to show my children love, patience, and respect. I want them to be good humans. Not because that's the right thing to do, but purely for selfish reasons. Seriously. I have to live with these people every single day for 18 years. Then, I plan on spending holidays and vacations with them and their friends and their families for the rest of my life. I assume I'll also want their help when I get old and need a ride to my granny hip-hop class.

If I raise a bunch of self-centered, lazy, disrespectful humans, that'll be a *huge* bummer for me. I want people around me who are kind and funny, sweet and interesting, loving and independent. See? *It's totally selfish.*

I'm always baffled when I hear parents jokingly comment their children are *a-holes*. I'm not talking about teenagers. *Believe me, I understand hormone surges result in temporary insanity.* But a 4-year-old? A 7-year-old? *Please tell me you're kidding.* If you're not kidding, please don't give up before releasing them into the world with the rest of us. What if I end up next to them on a long flight? Seriously. If *you* don't like your kids, what makes you think *I* want to hang out with them?

I'm not saying it's easy or you can change someone's core personality traits, or a super difficult child will magically turn into the most polite, compassionate, respectful kid on the planet. *But, please do not give up on them.* Everything you do can help at least a little, maybe even more than you dare to dream. If these chapters don't help at all, try a different book, a therapist, less sugar, a youth group, an earlier bedtime, a different school, an allergy test, more outside playtime, an occupational therapist, a new sport, music, a month-long device break, journaling, karate, more responsibilities at home, painting, molecular chemistry, less dairy, dance, meditation, or cooking.

Try fewer scheduled activities or maybe more downtime without TV or devices. Anything. Or try everything at once! *Joking.* But, maybe your *Monkey Gut* nudged at you as you read one of those options? If so, please try it. You will be grateful when you're 92 with your daughter playing her violin at your bedside, and you both muse about that short period of time when she was an *a-hole*.

Parenting with Your *Monkey Gut*

When I first became a mom, I read a lot of books on parenting. Most of these books got me amped up about their advice and recommendations. Then, after a couple of weeks, I stopped using the tools because they didn't work. Or, they worked with one son but backfired with another. I jumped from one parenting philosophy to another, always trusting *the experts* over my own instincts.

Have I mentioned I have four sons? They're very close in age, share the same genetics, same gender, same home-life, and the same socioeconomic background. Yet, they are all *very* different. They react differently to me, and I react differently to each of them.

How do I know if I'm doing things right?

Well, there is no *perfect* parent, and there is no *perfect* child - or *perfect* relationship. We all have different personalities, needs, abilities, hopes, and dreams.

 Everyone is unique, and as soon as you think you've figured them out, they change.

You might have a child who is far more difficult to parent than you ever imagined possible. You might have a child you struggle with because your personalities are so different or because you're so similar. Maybe you can't figure out how to connect with them or how to best help them. Maybe you're laid back and easygoing, but your child is strong-willed, with big emotional outbursts.

You're busy trying to keep everyone fed and safe and on time to their scheduled activities. *When do you have the time or energy to sit back with a cup of herbal tea and ask yourself what type of human you're trying to raise? Then, how do you find the tools and time to actually do it?*

In a recent Stretch Marks Retreat, Monica shared the weight of her parenting guilt. She felt terrible about the potential impact her depression and irritability had on her six-year-old daughter. With tears in her eyes, she revealed her fear of passing emotional baggage on to her daughter. At this point, several other women chimed in to say their daughters displayed similar behaviors at that age, though their mothers weren't depressed. Often, we assume our children's actions directly reflect our inept abilities, when they may well be 100% normal and healthy for the child's developmental stage. Don't be so quick to beat yourself up!

If that isn't tricky enough, you probably have a partner or an ex, or both. Chances are the other parent has their own ideas about what type of human *they* want to raise. What if you have different dreams for your children? Maybe your partner was super shy as a child. As a result, they may want your child to become social and popular. But, the popular kids bullied you, and you don't want your child joining that crowd. You two could inadvertently send very different messages to your kiddo.

Not only is it important to be clear with yourself about which character traits you want to encourage in your children, but it's also critical to see if you're on the same page as the rest of your parenting team.

Get that herbal tea ready because you're gonna take the next two minutes and figure out what type of child you want to have in your life for the next fifty years.

THE TOP FOUR

Remember your Top Five from the first chapter? Well, here we go again. This time though, it's about the kids, and there are only four. Scan through these characteristics and check the four you deem MOST important:

- [ ] Kind
- [ ] Generous
- [ ] Persistent
- [ ] Patient
- [ ] Resilient
- [ ] Compassionate
- [ ] Tenacious
- [ ] Humble
- [ ] Creative
- [ ] Courageous
- [ ] Passionate
- [ ] Honest
- [ ] Independent

☐ Empathetic
☐ Confident
☐ Other _____
☐ Other _____

If you had trouble choosing, finish this sentence:
Upon graduation, your child's high school advisor says to you, *Wow! How did you raise someone so...* _____
_____
_____.

Example: creative, kind, passionate, and independent
Example: confident, honest, tenacious, and resilient
Example: adventurous, patient, curious, and trustworthy

I'm not advocating you try to make a cookie-cutter *perfect* children. That would be creepy. No. What I'm suggesting is you *encourage* the Top Four qualities you deem most important. *This will make a big difference in your life.* When my four were younger, I plastered big cartoon-bubble posters all over their room. Each bubble had a different trait we'd talk about at bedtime. *Compassion. Kindness. Creativity.* The boys drew pictures on the bubble posters, depicting their interpretation of each trait. We made it no secret what qualities we most admire in others.

But *How* Do I Do It?

1. Encourage and compliment your Top Four traits when you see your child doing them naturally. Even when you notice just a *hint* of creativity, or kindness, comment on it. Let them overhear you speaking to someone else about what you noticed.

   Warning: Do not use a comparison between children as you do this. Compliments are only beneficial when said without insulting anyone else in the family. If you have one child who takes personal offense to any compliments about their siblings, do it one-on-one instead.

For instance, if you see an act of empathy, you might say, *Hey, I noticed you walked back to class with Sarah after those girls teased her. That impressed me and made me feel proud.*

 Giving more compliments and fewer criticisms will improve behavior a lot.

2. Model your Top Four traits every day. Model the characteristic you'd like to enhance and then talk about it in front of your child. For instance, if you want to model resilience, talk about a time you worked really hard at something, failed, and didn't give up. Maybe explain what you learned from the failure, and why you're glad you kept at it.

For instance, if you'd like to model humility, make sure your children see how you react to compliments from others. Then, talk about it later that day. Mention it during dinner or at bedtime. Explain to them *why* you responded the way you did.

How Will This Help Me?

Deciding your Top Four will:
1. Help you make better discipline decisions and give you more confidence in those decisions, *which, will make you more likely to follow through on your decisions.*
2. Help you explain your discipline decisions more clearly to your children, *which, I highly recommend you take the time to do.*

3. Help you communicate to your children what qualities your family values most. *Which, will make them more likely to exhibit those qualities.*
4. Help you consciously model those qualities yourself, *which, if you truly value them, will make you a better person too.*

Think about it. What's most important to you? What qualities would you most want to see in your children? Keeping those traits top of mind will increase the odds you'll encourage and reinforce those characteristics when you see them displayed. It doesn't happen magically. Some kiddos will need more constant reminders and acknowledgment than others. But, I promise it'll be worth the effort!

COMPETITION

The best parenting advice I ever read was how to stop sibling rivalry. Well, maybe not *stop*. That may be impossible. I'll say, *minimize their natural competitive tendencies.* The tools recommended by authors Adele Faber and Elaine Mazlish saved my sanity.

Most adults who've spent time with my boys, remark to me (often with surprise) how supportive and kind they are with one another. Each boy doesn't consider the success of one brother as a failure for himself. Instead, a win for one is a win for everyone. My husband, Jaimie, and I both grew up as the only child of a single mother. We saw families with lots of kids around us. We watched in awe at the opportunity to have full-time playmates, confidants, and sibling-cheerleaders. The idea of having four children grow up resenting one another or hurting one another emotionally or psychologically would break my heart.

For example, my boys love playing chess. My younger two often beat the older two now. Instead of this causing conflict, they high-five the winner when they lose a game. It's four boys ages 6-11 who get along, have fun together, and treat one another with respect and kindness...*about 95% of the time.*

This did not happen overnight, and it didn't happen by accident - or luck. It takes lots of encouragement and reinforcement. It takes both Jaimie and me constantly modeling what we feel is important, talking about what we value most, and not letting them get away with behavior we don't like. *It's a lot of work.* But, I'll gladly do it if it means I get to keep my sanity and have awesome humans around me for the next 60 years.

Competition brings out the best in products and the worst in people.
Faqimi Fauzi

I also totally mess up. I lose my cool. I am not perfect. But I will not give up because this isn't something you do for a week and you're all set. Nope. It's a constant thing. In fact, I'm sitting on a plane on our way to Ottawa. My 7-year-old just asked me for gum. I said yes and handed him the whole pack. He gave a piece to each of his brothers. Then, he took a piece for himself. I told him I liked how he gave all his brothers a piece *before* taking one for himself. *I thought that was very considerate and cool of you.*

Think of how often you talk about what you *don't* like or what they're doing wrong. Do you point out how a sibling did something faster or quieter or more respectfully? I feel like a coach all the time. *Seriously, how many times do I have to ask you to take your cereal bowl to the sink? Do not roll your eyes at me! Stop drumming on the hotel floor!* Sometimes, I feel like I'm speaking into the vacuum of deep space. How often do you remind your child where the dirty clothes belong? How often do you find wet towels on the floor? How often do you tell them to turn down the volume on their electric bass amplifier? *Can nobody in this house hear my voice!?* Clearly it doesn't happen overnight. All I'm asking is you don't stop trying, for their sake and your sake.

Lesson 1: Fair Schmair

Fair doesn't mean each child gets the *same* thing or the *same* amount of something. Do you ever hear, *Daaaaaad, her piece of cake has more frosting than mine! He got the iPad longer than me!* This constant screeching for fairness would drive me nuts. Honestly, my boys don't say these words. They know, after years of living with me, such a response would not result in a happy reaction from mom. Sometimes, having four children actually makes discipline decisions easier. Imagine if you had double the number of children you currently have. What if all of them threw a tantrum simultaneously? What if they all ignored you every time you asked a question? If you let one little thing slide, you're in for an avalanche of problems.

Here's something to try: each child gets what *they* need when *they* need it. Michael needs a new backpack. Danny needs help with his homework. Evan needs some alone time with mommy. Christopher needs to Skype with his friend who just moved out of the country. Each request or need is individual and has *nothing* to do with his or her siblings. I'd drive myself bonkers if I tried to make sure everyone had the exact same amount of syrup on their pancakes!

When this came up the first several hundred times, I'd say, *If you want more of something, ask ME. Don't worry about what your brother has. I may not always say yes. But, whatever he has has NOTHING to do with you.* The kids eventually caught on. Comparing themselves to each other, in an attempt to get more stuff or more attention, simply didn't work. Now, it doesn't even occur to them to compare pieces of cake. If they want more, they can ask me. I may say, *Sure, you can have another piece.* Or, I may say, *Actually, you had a milkshake at lunch, so you're good with that, buddy.*

Another benefit: children can learn to ask themselves what they want. *Wait, do I care about a new jacket? Do I want one because my brother has one? Actually, I don't like syrup. Can I have jelly instead?*

What kind of precedent are we setting for these children if they think life is always going to treat them fairly? What happens when they get the crappy cubicle by the bathroom at their first job? What happens when their math professor gives twice as much homework as their roommate's professor? Or they lose the big game even though they played their hardest?

The real question is this: *What do you want them to learn? How do you want your kids to react to unfair circumstances? What happens when they encounter all the unfairness in the real world? Will they be prepared?* Your home is like a life-laboratory. It's the training ground. It's where they get to experiment, practice, and learn the skills they'll need in the real world. If you're unsure about a parenting decision, ask yourself, *what's the lesson here?*

Have no fear of perfection - you'll never reach it.
Salvador Dali

Lesson 2: Winning is Only Temporary

How do you reduce the blow of losing? Explain that winning is temporary. It's highly unlikely your child will forever remain the tallest, or fastest, or best*est* at anything. Even the Guinness Book of World Records is revised and republished every year. Most parenting books recommend focusing on trying your best instead of who won. *That's great.* They say we should focus on tenacity and grit. *So true.* But, I'd recommend you take it a step further by reminding both winner and loser no win is permanent or everlasting.

Yes, your sister might be faster than you, or better at cooking scrambled eggs, or taller, but that may change.

You're right, your brother can do that skate trick and you can't quite do it yet. Keep working on it and who knows what might happen!

Even when my boys were very little, I'd use this tactic. *Yes, Danny can run faster than anyone in our family. Right now. Maybe in a few years, Evan will be the fastest.*

Side Note: Make sure to celebrate the win first. You don't have to make a huge deal of it or do it in front of everyone. But allowing for celebration is important. *I'm not recommending you throw a big party because your child won the class spelling bee.* Not at all. I mean their accomplishments get acknowledged. Maybe it's a family toast at dinner, a special trip to the ice cream shop, or a call to grandma to tell her the news.

Both my husband and I grew up feeling like we could not celebrate our *wins*. He was encouraged to hide or downplay his accomplishments, for fear they might make other family members feel bad. My parents were wonderfully supportive of and confident in my abilities. So much so, it sucked the excitement out of the win. To this day, my father responds to my *wins* with a bigger challenge. It looks something like this: *Of course, you got a book contract! So, when do you start your law degree?*

As an adult, I fully understand this is his way of showing his confidence in me. He is not surprised by any of my accomplishments because he has faith in my ability to do almost anything. *This is good, right?* Yes and no. If you do this with your kiddos, remember every child can use a good old, *Wow, that is so great! I'm so impressed and proud.* Otherwise, you can end up creating an achievement junkie. While this is not a terrible thing, your child might spend five years on an advanced degree they don't even want. *Ahem, yes that was me.*

Lesson 3: Winning Doesn't Make You *Better*

Another perspective that helps dampen competition between siblings is the reminder that winning does not make you more valuable as a human being. If you're faster or taller or can jump higher, it means at this specific point in time, you are faster or taller or can jump higher. It means one thing, at one point in time. *That's great.* But, that's all it means. Being fastest doesn't make you more valuable than your siblings.

 What we value most in this family is that you are kind, tenacious, generous, and creative. *(Insert your own Top Four.)*

So much of a child's competitive behavior with their siblings comes from a deep need to make sure they're getting the love and attention they need. It's basic human nature. Survival. Love your children by keeping them safe, listening to them, feeding them healthy foods, teaching them valuable skills, and hugging them daily. Tell your children how you feel about them with your spoken words, your eye contact, and lots of smiles. When they feel loved and valued by your words and your actions, they may not get as upset the next time their little sister eats the last bowl of the *good* cereal.

Also, when our children feel upset or disappointed about one of our parenting decisions, Jaimie and I remind them it's not our job to make them happy. We explain to them *over and over*; it's our job to teach them to become good humans. We want to keep them safe and healthy. We want to guide them so they will become independent and responsible young men. We want them to figure out how they can combine their interests, talents, and abilities to help solve a problem in the world. Specifically, any problem they feel especially passionate about.

KEY PARENTING TAKEAWAYS

Your Top Four:
1. Talk about your Top Four in front of your children.
2. Use your Top Four to support your discipline decisions.
3. Encourage your Top Four through praise and modeling.

Competition:
1. Winning is awesome, but temporary.
2. Winning doesn't reflect your value as a human.
3. True fairness is each child getting what *they* need when *they* need it.

Never yell at your kids.
Lean in real close and whisper,
it's much scarier.
Anonymous

Chapter Five

SUPERMODEL PARENTING

It is our choices, Harry, that show what we truly are.
Far more than our abilities.
Harry Potter and the Chamber of Secrets by J.K. Rowling

You Own Everything

Literally. Nothing is *theirs*. You own it. If it's *their* birthday, and *they* receive gifts, then *they* get to play with them. But, you're the owner. I find this philosophy immediately stops many potential arguments. I expect my children to share, treat our property with respect, and abide by whatever rules we've determined. Here's the kicker: you must be willing to remove the toy or game if they're not following the rules you've set. This part is key. *I know it is not easy.* If it was easy, everyone would do it, and we would never hear a child whine, *But, mom pleeeeeeease!*

This is where your Top Four come into play. Unless your Top Four are selfish, obnoxious, impatient, and disrespectful, then you must <u>stand firm</u>. How do you show them you're serious? Try donating a toy or a device to *someone who will appreciate it more, or someone who will respect their parents' rules.* Do this once every six months, and I'll bet your child will listen up the next time you set a limit or make a rule they don't like. I'm serious. If you don't try it, I will take your Netflix subscription away! *I'm kidding.* Actually, if you don't try it, you might find your life becomes an endless battle of wills.

Be A Supermodel

No. I don't mean smoke cigarettes and eat a strict diet of kale and quinoa. *(If you're a supermodel, I apologize for being presumptuous. Maybe you eat greasy burgers and key lime pie and still look like that?!)* What I mean is you become *super* at *modeling* the very traits and qualities you'd like to encourage in your children.

You'll earn your child's respect by treating *them* with respect. Give lots of compliments and hugs, and you'll get more in return. This does not mean giving them anything they want. It doesn't mean allowing them to do whatever their friends are allowed to do. It means modeling to them how you'd like to be treated in return. It means modeling how you'd like them to behave.

I wanted my kids to love books and reading like I do. So, not only do I try to read in front of my kids, I let them *catch* me reading. For example, they'll walk into a room and see me alone, reading. I want them to eat healthy food. So, I hide my milk chocolate with the toffee chunks in the freezer. *Don't judge!*

When I'm doing something I don't want them to emulate, I explain *why* I'm doing it. Maybe I'm on my phone at a restaurant, or I cross a street where there is no crosswalk. I'll explain, *I'm sending grandma a text message because she had a doctor's appointment today and I want her to know we are thinking about her.* Or, *I'm walking us across the street here because it's safer than at the corner right now.*

Chunk Yourself

Do you ever feel like you need a time-out? If you're like me, you might benefit from several time-outs a day. I need a few minutes to breathe, calm down, and adjust my perspective a bit. Sometimes, I realize I'm about to cry and scream into a pillow because of some little nuisance that never would have bothered me if... *I hadn't woken up 12 times the night before, sat in pee on the toilet seat (after showering), reminded Chris to please take his cereal bowl to the sink for the 157th time, found a pile of rocks in my purse, stubbed my pinky toe on a skate board and then found I had no clean shirts because I forgot to put the laundry into the drier the night before.*

That's when I need to give myself a little time-out. I need to chill or risk bursting a blood vessel. In our house, a time-out for the kids includes a one-on-one talk about whatever happened, why we are upset about it, and what behavior we expect in the future. We call it *getting chunked*. I'm not sure how this term came to be exactly. But, it happens quite regularly. Someone gets *chunked*. I'd like to encourage you not only to give yourself periodic time-outs, but also to *chunk* yourself. Do it in front of your children. *Chunk* yourself when you're doing or saying something you would typically *chunk* your kids about.

To *Chunk* Yourself: Explain what happened, why you're not happy with your reaction or behavior, and what you will try to do the next time.

Maybe you overreacted? *I do this often.* Maybe you catch yourself texting while driving? Or you gossip about someone in front of your child? Anytime you find yourself doing something you'd like them *not* to emulate, *chunk* yourself. Maybe you'd like to foster patience, but you're acting super impatient? *Chunk* yourself right then and there. *Wow, I'm feeling really impatient right now. I need a time-out. I'm going to step outside and take ten long deep breaths. I'll be back in a few minutes.*

No Means No

It is easier to stand firm when you're clear *why* you said no in the first place. Think of your Top Four. Did you say no because it conflicts with one of the qualities you value most? Great. Then, you can feel confident you're making the right choice for you and your family. If it wasn't based on anything you feel strongly about, then read on and remember, it's OK to change your mind.

Changing Your Mind

This is important to model for your children as well. The best leaders are the ones who adjust their behavior and decisions as a result of new information. Companies that don't evolve with the times wither and die. Being secure enough in yourself and your decisions means you can also change them when you determine a different course is better.

It looks like this; *I was going to let you stay up late for a movie night tonight. But, now I see you're becoming disrespectful and violent with your brother. I think you're overtired and I realize we've all had a long day. We will see how tomorrow goes. If everyone is kind and respectful, we can stay up later and watch the movie tomorrow night.* Done. No arguments. Further arguments equal more days without the movie night.

 **Rewarding behavior with compliments, smiles, eye contact, and hugs is far more effective than rewarding with iPad time, toys, or desserts.**

Ladies & Gentlemen

Another great piece of advice from my doula Carmen: *refer to your children as ladies and/or gentlemen.* Even if they're tiny and don't yet know the meaning of these words, it makes an impact. I'll say, *Gentlemen, it's time to put on your shoes and get in the car, please. Gentlemen, let's clean up this living room before our friends come over.* Psychologically, this helps both the parents and the kids. It reminds everyone you're expecting respectful, mature behavior. In our family, *being a gentleman* means making eye contact while introducing yourself, saying thank you when anyone hands you anything, saying please whenever you ask for something, and responding verbally when asked a question. *What would it mean in your family?*

By the way, it drives me crazy when my kids don't respond to me, aloud, with actual words. I tell them often; I need to hear words in response to a question. Grunts, sound effects, and mmmhmmm's do not count. Some days I have to get up and announce, *Can somebody please talk to me!?* Remember my recommendation about 20 minutes of daily adult female conversation? This is important. I think this is why so many women I know watch old *Friends* episodes on Netflix. It serves as a mini substitute for adult conversation and it's funny.

Notes on Discipline

1. It's never too late to change the rules and expectations in your family. Get serious about your role as the boss. In fact, the sooner the better. Changing the rules with a hormone-laden teenager? *No thanks.* Do it now before your kids are six inches taller than you and their girlfriends post half-naked selfies on Instagram. *Yikes!*
   ✓ For example: *You know I've been thinking about last weekend. There was a lot of arguing, attitude, and disrespectful behavior. It made me feel sad. From now on,*

I want all of us to show kindness and consideration for each other. Not only will it be more pleasant for all of us, but it'll make me want to plan more fun stuff to do on the weekends.

2. If you're a tough cookie now, parenting will be a lot easier down the road. It's back to that same delayed gratification concept. Do the hard work now, and you'll reap the rewards later. The more consistent you can be, the less time it'll take for everyone to get on board. If you're clear and consistent for the next three months, I'll bet you will see a huge difference in your family. (If three months sounds entirely too daunting, take it day by day.)

You can do this.

The Flip Side

Almost all character traits have a flip side. Maybe you have trouble relating to one of your children because they are so different from you? You might feel upset or worried about a characteristic your child naturally has in abundance. Your kiddo might be so shy and quiet, you worry they'll have trouble finding friends or won't have a happy social life as they get older. Or your child might be overly social and you fear they are not paying enough attention to school work or other responsibilities.

It may help to ask yourself this: *What's the flipside? How might this natural tendency help them in adulthood? In what types of situations is this trait useful? What sort of professions value people who have this quality?*

Being confident can be wonderful. However, the flip side is it may appear cocky or obnoxious. People who are overly cautious may protect themselves from heartache and disappointment on one side, but miss out on opportunities or experiences. Those who are creative might lose track of time, forget appointments, or misplace their keys. There are pluses and minuses to almost any trait.

I believe my job is helping my children understand where their natural traits and abilities will serve them best. A creative daydreamer might not be a fantastic stock analyst, where details and time-dependent decisions are critical. A super logical, assertive, outspoken person might not work best at helping battered women try to rebuild their lives.

Actually, I'm wrong. They could totally help battered women by working on Capitol Hill as an advocate for women's rights. This planet needs a variety of skills, abilities, and personality types. There's space for all of us to flourish. For instance, my good friend Delmy loves auditing. She's a certified public accountant and can spend hours describing a current accounting project. She says it's like figuring out a giant puzzle and feels amazing when all the numbers line up just right. Or there's my friend Andy, who not only loves to cook, but loves teaching my children to cook. Chef Andy enjoys taking the time to shop for the best, fresh ingredients. He loves prepping and cooking while I would happily turn over my kitchen *and a kid or two* to anyone who'd eliminate cooking from my life!

Then there's my friend Karima, a sergeant at the L.A.P.D., whose job requires her to deal with awful people and scary scenarios. The situations she's seen in her line of work would leave me clinically depressed. I'd have nightmares every night while Karima would rather lose her left arm in a freak bowling accident than travel the country with my husband and four children.

These wonderful friends have skills and abilities I admire and respect greatly. Thankfully, we all have different talents and interests. When each of us spends our time and energy in an area that benefits from our natural strengths, it helps everyone.

When you're getting paid for something you'd do for free, or when someone asks your advice on a topic you'd happily discuss for hours, you know you're in your element. You're happier, calmer, and probably doing a much better job than anyone else would do in the same position.

KEY DISCIPLINE TAKEAWAYS

1. Remember, *you* own everything. *Teaching the responsibility of ownership is great. But, if they're not respecting your parental rules, then maybe they don't deserve it.*
2. Be a Supermodel. *Be an example of the traits you want to encourage.*
3. Chunk yourself. *Show them you're not perfect, and you're always trying to improve yourself.*

Having one child makes you a parent.
Having two kids makes you a referee.
David Frost

Chapter Six

ISN'T THIS SUPPOSED TO BE FUN?

*On the night you were born, the moon smiled with such
wonder that the stars peeked in to see you and the night
wind whispered, 'Life will never be the same.'*
On the Night You Were Born by Nancy Tillman

Sometimes, I forget to have fun. I have a lot of kids. I get
caught up in organizing their activities, refereeing their
interactions, and managing the household. I forget to enjoy
them. I forget to have fun. People say, *Oh it goes so fast! Enjoy
it!* Yeah, sure. *How am I supposed to do that when I can't even
find my two matching shoes so I don't have to leave the house in
my socks?*

Making time and figuring out simple ways to bring fun
into your life as a parent is truly priceless. I don't really like to
cook or have them with me during errands, but I do love crafty
stuff. I like helping them with their homework. I like reading to
them, doing puzzles, or drawing. *What do you enjoy doing that
might be fun to do with your kiddos? What can you teach them that*

55

you already like to do? Kids often like what you like. Even when they don't act like it, they want to be with you. So, if you love puzzles, or knitting, or surfing… try teaching them.

Family Customs are another fantastic way to incorporate some joy in the busy land of household chores and responsibilities. *What new traditions or customs can you start in your family?*

Here are some you're welcome to steal:

Family Toasts: Kids like toasting even more than grown-ups. You can put water in some wine glasses to make it more festive. Each member of the family takes their turn toasting something they appreciate about their day, their week, or just their life. We like to say one *small* thing and one *big* thing.

Kid Example: *I'm thankful for that really cool spider I found in the backyard today and for my family all being together tonight.*

My Example: *I'm grateful the spider was not inside my house, and I'm grateful all my boys are kind-hearted and supportive of one another.*

Family Nights: You can take a vote and institute something like Spaghetti & Meatball Mondays, Walk in the Park Wednesdays, Board Game Fridays, or Movie Night Sundays. I always remember my mom talking about how her family had tacos on Friday nights. It seems so simple, right? Kids may not remember that $800 trip to Disneyland or the expensive Lego set you bought for their 10th birthday, but they *will* remember the stuff you did regularly.

What do you remember most from your childhood? Let me rephrase, what do you remember *fondly* from your childhood?

For example: I was very close with my ex-husband's family. We took many trips and spent many holidays together, over the ten years they were part of my life. You know what I remember most fondly? How my ex-mother-in-law would run her fingers through my hair when I sat next to her on the sofa. I remember thumb-wrestling my ex-father-in-law as he sat in his big brown recliner. Those are two of my most precious memories.

It's often the activities that cost nothing, happen regularly, and get you laughing and smiling that'll make a mark in your child's memory. I remember eating dinner at a big wooden oval-shaped dining table at my neighbor's house, with their three awesomely loud and boisterous kids. We'd laugh so hard one of us would inevitably snort milk out of our noses. Painful and gross *now*, absolutely fantastic and hilarious *then*. It was the best.

Side note: I often jokingly tell the mom of that family (who had a perpetually revolving mountain of laundry on her sofa), it's her *fault* I have so many children. Her house was always so dang fun. So loud. So exciting. It was the roller coaster to my cruise-controlled Toyota Corolla childhood. My house was safe, dependable, and very, very quiet. In her house, people either screamed with laughter or screamed with frustration. I don't remember anything in between. It was fabulous and I couldn't get enough.

Much later, after I'd had my third son, I called this neighborhood mom and told her I'd successfully recreated the loud and wild environment I'd so cherished in her home as a child.

The Good News: My house is loud and fun.

The Bad News: I'm now the parent in the loud and fun house, which is very different than being one of the kids in the fun house. I also live here full-time. I'm no longer a visitor who can return to her quiet, calm house.

A few years ago, I rented a small office in the back of a physical therapy center a couple of miles from my home. I needed a quiet space to work and think. My friends thought I was crazy. *It was the best money I've ever spent.*

Your Sanity is Priceless.

Circle Compliments: This tradition is helpful when two or more family members are consistently at odds with one another. Everyone sits in a circle and says one thing they admire or like about the family member to their left. If you have more time, or the children are enjoying the game, have each family member give one compliment to *all* the other members of the family.

I like doing this right before bedtime. It's a nice way to end the day. Everyone appreciates hearing nice things about themselves and when the compliment comes from a sibling's mouth, even better. *Especially when it comes from a sibling you think hates you.* I always find the tension in the house goes down a notch after we do a round of Circle Compliments.

In almost all of these examples, you can sneak in some easy Top Four encouragements. The kids will notice what you're grateful for and what you focus on most at the end of the day. For example: *I'm so grateful my children are creative, kind, and care about other people.*

Focus on The Positive

Do you feel you're constantly *chunking* your kids' behavior? All day long, you're correcting them and calling them out on something they've said or done wrong. Try this: for every three times you *chunk* them, find one thing to compliment. Even if it's a minor thing. Find something. Be genuine. And remember sarcasm has no place in compliments.

The Bad Example: *Wow, you have on a clean shirt for once!*

The Good Example: *I like the way you're all dressed and ready in clean clothes. You look great.*

Bonus points if you give one compliment for every *chunk*. Figure out your current ratio. Do you *chunk* ten times for every one compliment? See if you can get your ratio to 5:1 instead of 10:1. Any little bit helps. I believe you'll see a difference in your kid's behavior and attitude. Even the toughest kiddos seek your praise and acknowledgment.

If you can admit you almost never give a genuine compliment, start with one a day. Preface it by acknowledging, *I realize I never say this, but you should know I'm very proud of how you always encourage the other kids on your soccer team.*

Know Your Audience

You are human. Since your children will probably deal with humans for the rest of their lives, it's good practice for them to understand as much as they can. Not only is nobody perfect, but everyone is different. We have different feelings and moods. We get grouchy and tired. We have different personalities and preferences. I want my children to learn to *read* people's moods and personalities. The best place to learn how to do this is in your life-laboratory.

I might say, *Hey guys, remember how I didn't sleep great last night? Well, my patience is super thin. I'm gonna try to be calm. But just know, I'm very sensitive right now.* Or, *Guys, dad had a stressful photo shoot today, so let's give him some extra help when he gets home.* The key here is to prompt this ahead of time, so it's a learning experience and not a correction after the fact.

Children can understand while it's not their fault you're in a mood, they'd best stand clear and be on alert. Learning how to navigate your family member's moods and personalities will benefit your kiddos when they leave your life-lab and enter real life. For instance, my boys know what types of things bug dad most, but maybe don't bother me so much and vice versa.

For example, I'm not a fan of potty talk. Or toots. Or burps. For the boys, and often dad, these things are *hilarious*. When Danny was about 4, he got ahold of my label maker (an impulse buy at Staples). One morning, I found the following words posted all over the house: PEE, POOP, TOILET, PENUS, and TOWEL.

As they say in the comedy world, *know your audience.*

TECHNOLOGY

Remember the old-school telephone mounted on the kitchen wall of your childhood home? That fancy device was patented in 1876 and remained virtually the same for over one hundred years. Then, it became cordless. That was a big deal. *Woohoo! I'm not stuck to the kitchen wall anymore!*

Now, technology upgrades happen overnight while we sleep and our phones function as computers, stereos, calculators, books, and TVs. It blows my mind. Our cell phones give us access to almost every bit of information available on the planet. All of it! Recently, I heard a comic point out calling these magical devices *phones* is like calling a Lexus convertible a *cup holder.*

Technology is now one of the biggest challenges in the world of parenting. These tiny magical devices have changed the world and our children are tech-geniuses. As of 2016, over two billion people spend an average of two hours and fifteen minutes a day on social media sites. But that's nothing. Our children have us beat by a mile. Common Sense Media found teenagers average nine hours per day and tweens six hours a day on social media sites. Nope, these hours do not include time spent on homework. There are very few things I can think of I'd like to do for nine hours a day. *Besides sleep of course.*

How do they even have that many hours available in a day? I can barely find four minutes to brush my teeth every morning!

Young children watch videos of other people's children opening gifts. It's called unboxing. *Have you heard of this?* If your children watch these videos, they are not alone. In 2014, CNN reported YouTube viewers were watching almost six billion hours of *unboxing* content each month. Also popular are first-person shooter games. *Yes, like Fortnite.* Guess how much money they're making. With 45 million active players, *Fortnite* pulls in over $300 million dollars every month. *Three. Hundred. Million.*

While Internet Gaming Disorder is not yet an official diagnosis, you might find it interesting to know the typical signs of 'addiction': a preoccupation with technology, withdrawal symptoms when not using technology, loss of interest in other activities or hobbies, using technology as a way to escape from feelings or reality, and lying about the use of technology.

There are loads of recommendations regarding physical safety, inappropriate content, and emotional issues related to social media and video games. But, those are topics for a different book. I want to stay focused on how to make your life easier and happier. How do social media or video games affect your life as a parent? *Would your life be easier if you had less conflict or guilt about devices?* If so, try one of the following rules, and see if there's a difference in your anxiety or frustration levels.

Technology Rules:

Explain to your kiddos what you count as screen time. *For instance, homework, educational content, or family movie night doesn't count as screen time.*

Set a per-day limit and find an easy way to measure it. *For instance, setting a timer or having a fixed time each day for devices. If it's a game like Fortnite, you can measure by the number of battles they complete.*

Establish electronic curfews. *For instance, one hour before bedtime the phone goes into a charger in the kitchen.*

Set up occasional device-free days. *Ideally, do something fun during these days. It can be a nice reminder you can have fun even if you're not posting about it.*

KEY TECHNOLOGY TAKEAWAYS

1. Decide on technology rules based on what *you* want for *your* family.
2. Follow through on your plan. Change it when necessary.
3. Always remember, you're the boss, and you own everything.

My kid is turning out just like me.
Well played, karma. Well-played.
Anonymous

PART III

GET UNSTUCK

Chapter Seven

THE ASK MINDSET: *WEAR A COWBOY HAT*

And now here is my secret, a very simple secret:
It is only with the heart that one can see rightly;
what is essential is invisible to the eye.
The Little Prince by Antoine de Saint-Exupéry

In the past, I analyzed everything. I even analyzed my dreams for the future. I'd uncover every reason a plan would be unsuccessful. For several years, I managed to sabotage every good idea that popped into my mind. This left me very frustrated. Finally, the epiphany came while watching my husband, Jaimie, jump headfirst into founding a charity. He had zero experience in the nonprofit world and no assurances his idea could even work.

This did not stop him.

Instead of waiting around until he had all the answers, he poured his heart and soul into *finding* a way to make it happen.

It wasn't always easy, but he did it. He made something real. Something good. Not only did he impact people's lives in an amazing way, he felt proud, useful, and happy.

I spent several years trying to pin down what I wanted to do *next*. Once I wasn't completely absorbed with the responsibilities of having young children, I craved feeling relevant again outside my home. But, I floated around, jumping from idea to idea. I researched and analyzed each new plan until I killed it. I found problems with every idea. I worried I'd waste a bunch of time or money. I had no extra of either to waste.

Then, one afternoon Jaimie and I argued for the 80th time about him taking a trip for his charity. I felt like his ability to pursue a passion project made it impossible for me to pursue my own. This was a *Baloney Belief*. Because, during that last fight, I realized Jaimie had the *secret sauce* answer. As illogical and scattered as it seemed, his approach worked. He listened to his *Monkey Gut*.

Instead of doubting himself or questioning everything, he made phone calls, sent emails, and got our kids involved. He filled up carts with holiday gifts and drove to hospitals every single holiday. They often turned him away. Receptionists looked at him funny because he was doing something that hadn't been done before. *We only accept gifts at Christmastime.* They'd call their supervisors. Some would reluctantly take the gifts and send him on his way, while others would refuse the gifts entirely.

He did not give up. After consistent badgering and volunteering, he slowly built trust with several Los Angeles hospitals. Three years later, he did his first photo shoot with a sweet 10-year-old boy named Aaron, who was fighting for his life. Jaimie and his partner Jesse made Aaron into his favorite superhero, the Incredible Hulk. Jaimie's dedication, his ability to pursue his dream regardless of a clear plan, a proven path, worked. My approach, on the other hand, resulted in a very grouchy and frustrated momma.

My Story: A Passion Project

I wanted to listen to my *Monkey Gut*. I asked myself, *what would I do at this point in my life if I was guaranteed success? What would I do if I had a Jaimie mindset?* My answer: *start a school.* I immediately texted a friend I thought might be interested in becoming a partner in the project. Her response was "F-YES!" We spent the next nine months researching educational approaches, meeting with teachers, and touring other schools.

I started with one small step: a text to my friend Monica.

I chose something that interested and excited me – education.

I shared my plan only with those who would support and encourage me: Jaimie, my sister, my mom, and my dad.

Monica and I created a mission, a business plan, and educational guidelines. We flew to Reno and San Francisco for our research. We met with experts, teachers, and administrators. It was thrilling. I knew raising funds, securing a location, building a curriculum, and hiring a stellar team of teachers would take years.

After nine months of work on our project, I realized my Top Five might *not* be fulfilled by starting a school. I wouldn't be able to spend much time with family. I wouldn't be able to travel. And by the time the school opened, my children would be too old to attend it! Maybe there was a different way to have my Top Five Priorities in my life.

A New Dream

I determined I wanted to travel with my family, hire tutors for math and literacy, and explore the world. This was the best way to get all my Top Five into my life. So, I set off in a new direction. I was willing to change course because I finally realized there were other options, possibilities I didn't even know existed.

I never would have realized my new dream if I hadn't taken that detour. This new road I'm on wasn't even visible to me at the time. I had to get on the *Start a School Highway* first. I had to drive down that road for a bit. Then, I could finally see all the possible exits available to me. The road I was on before, did not connect to the *Travel with a Musical Interstate*. Sometimes you have to take a detour. Often, it's totally worth it.

My new dream involved travel and a daily life that changes constantly. Waking up at the same time, making lunches, and driving kids to school would be no more. A life of adventure, exploration, and a completely different approach to education satisfied so many of my Top Five at that time: travel, family, health, education, and financial security.

There is a voice inside of you that whispers all day long,
"I feel that this is right for me, I know that this is wrong."
No teacher, preacher, parent, friend or wise man
can decide what's right for you -
Just listen to the voice that speaks inside.
Shel Silverstein

Your Turn

What do you want? Deep down. For real. Not what would make you happy for the next hour or two. But, in your core, what do you need most in the world?

Which area would make the biggest difference to your life if it was greatly improved? Your health? Career? Finances? Relationships? Social life? Which one stirs your *Monkey Gut?* Let's go with that one for now.

Now, in that area of your life, which one of the following applies to you?

A. You have no idea what you want.
B. You know what you want. But, you think it's impossible.
C. You believe you shouldn't want it because it is greedy or obnoxious.

Finding What You Want

You Gotta Feel It

Try to describe what you want in this particular area of your life in **broad** terms and **feeling** words. This part is critical. Don't skip this. While many self-help books direct you to focus on *specifics*, I want you to focus on *feelings*.

For Example:

Career: Instead of saying, *I want to be a best-selling author and travel the world speaking at conferences,* you could say, *I want to be in a creative atmosphere, work with fantastic people, inspire and enrich the lives of others, feel intellectually stimulated, and have the flexibility and resources to travel with my family.*

Relationship: Instead of saying, *I want a man who works in finance, loves Jazz, and lives in New York City,* you could say, *I want to be with someone who is kind and loving, fun and ambitious, someone who makes me feels safe, loved, and appreciated every day.*

Write it out or say it aloud while driving to work. Try turning off the radio or news the next time you're traveling alone and see what pops into your mind. It may surprise you. Marco is tough to hear when the news is blaring on about what violent and disturbing events occurred over the weekend. Get quiet and listen.

There are no right answers; only answers right for *you*.

Here you are, witnessing your very own memorial service. Don't worry. You lived the most incredible life and died peacefully in your sleep at the age of 104. Your best friend is about to deliver your eulogy and says: (Fill in the blanks.)

The Eulogy

Although we will all miss her dearly, we can take solace knowing she lived an incredible life and was one of the happiest people I've ever known. She spent so much of her time doing what she loved most which was_____ and

_____

_____.

She was surrounded by those she loved most like _____ and _____.

She was incredibly happy when she accomplished her dream of _____

_____.

I will always remember her as a woman who was _____, _____, and _____.

Once you've filled in the eulogy blanks above, you will have a good idea which traits and actions rank highest on your list. These are what you value most. So, how much of your time, energy and resources do you spend on the activities and people you listed above? How often do you act in a way that corresponds to the qualities you listed?

Right now, what percentage of your time, energy, and resources do you spend on what is most important to you?

10%   25%   50%   75%   90%

What's your goal percentage?

Wear A Cowboy Hat

There are SO many examples of people with less experience, fewer resources, and suffering from more health issues who already live the life you seek. Life coach and best-selling author Marcia Wieder gives one of my favorite tips: wear a symbol of what you want.

For instance, if you're an accountant in Detroit, but dream of owning a cattle ranch in Texas, buy some boots and a hat. Wear them. See yourself as the rancher you wish to be.

Silly, right? But, what's the harm in trying if it gets you moving in the right direction? I tried her approach and here is what happened: I wanted to be on an island. I was sick of driving in traffic. Sick of superficial L.A. So, I went on a little shopping spree. *Ironic, I know.* I had a deeper purpose, I promise. I began wearing long flowing dresses and resort-type beachwear instead of my normal jeans or workout clothes. I looked as if I already lived on a tropical island.

Not only did I feel better, but I got a ton of compliments. Maybe I was smiling more. Or maybe I just looked out of place at the Culver City Market. I thought the experiment was going well. In the two years before this, I'd told Jaimie, *No more traveling for work!* It was just too hard for me with four kiddos in tow. I couldn't do it anymore. So, when my *Escape from LA* plan began, I told him, *Hey, if anyone calls to offer you a job in Hawaii, I'm game.* He assured me the only movie filming in Hawaii already had a photographer on board and he would never try to swoop in and knock someone else off a job. I told him, *Ok. I get it. But, sometimes plans change. I'm up for some time on an island, just so you know.*

Two weeks later, my husband received a job offer for the film shooting in Hawaii. We all spent five weeks living like locals in Oahu. Later, we discovered the original photographer had only ever planned to work the London portion of the film. It was a win for everyone.

Perhaps it was a complete coincidence. Who knows? I'm not guaranteeing this always works or it works instantaneously. But, it's free, easy, and can be a simple first step towards changing your life. Try your own version of the Hawaii Experiment. *Where do you want to go? What surprise would you like to receive?* I also used some tricks from Chapter 12, so please keep reading!

Delete It

Every time you catch yourself thinking or saying something negative:

1. Notice it.
2. Think "DELETE THAT PLEASE!"
3. Then, think or say aloud what you wish were true instead.

The next time you say "Argh, I'm always misplacing my keys!" Notice it. Think *Delete that please.* (I highly recommend you say it like a robot or in a British accent for added fun.) Then, think or say aloud, *I'm so grateful I always know where everything is whenever I need it.*

When you think, *Jeez I'm so out of shape, I just CANNOT stop eating all this crappy food!* Notice it. Delete it. Think, *I'm so grateful I'm strong and healthy.*

Yes, this is a mind game. It works because it rewires your brain. You may not even realize how often you think terrible thoughts about yourself. Each time you think or say something negative about yourself, your brain seeks future experiences to prove you right. You're brainwashing yourself to continue experiencing the same events, experiences, and people. Turn it upside-down and try brainwashing yourself into something new.

Pick Two

What if you cannot think of even one thing you want? Ok then, what are you *pretty good* at? Pick two of your interests or abilities and focus the majority of your time, resources and energy in *that* direction. Don't worry about the *how* quite yet; just focus on the *what*. Scott Adams used this strategy with fabulous results. He is the creator of *Dilbert* and a best-selling author worldwide.

In my case, I can draw better than most people, but I'm hardly an artist. And I'm not any funnier than the average stand-up comedian who never makes it big, but I'm funnier than most people. The magic is that few people can draw well and write jokes.
It's the combination of the two that makes what I do so rare.
Scott Adams

Scott is now a millionaire 75 times over.

What skills and talents do you have? What would your friends say you're really good at? Which of these activities would you gladly do *just for fun?*

It always helps to understand yourself better, right? Sometimes, you're too close to see yourself clearly. Which side of each pairing below appeals to you at this point in your life?

Working in a group vs. working alone

Big picture projects/ideas vs. planning, details, and follow through work

Physical, hands-on work vs. mental, problem-solving work

Creative and open-ended jobs vs. clearly defined and structured jobs

Many short projects all at once vs. one big long-term project

The Opposite Game

Do you want to be an IRS accountant working undercover for the Taliban? Do you want to be in a relationship with a selfish, arrogant jerk? Do you want to have friends who leave you feeling insecure and unsupported? No? See, you already know so many things you do not want to *do, be,* or *have* in your life! This is a good start. You think I'm joking, but it is a great way to begin. Identify everything you *know* you don't want in your life. Then, turn it inside-out and you'll see more clearly what you *do* want in your life.

For instance, I don't do well with the same schedule day in and day out. I also don't like being far from the beach or mountains. I don't like being in freezing weather with gray skies every day. I don't like being isolated from daily social interaction with other adults. I also don't like projects that are too easy, repetitive, or quick.

So, how might I turn that inside out? *I want to live close to a warm, beautiful beach, surrounded by fun, kind, supportive friends, and do something I love and enjoy every day.*

MINI-HOMEWORK ASSIGNMENT (5 minutes)

1. What THREE words or phrases are you deleting from your negative self talk?
2. List FIVE of your *pretty good* skills or talents.
3. Write out what you want in broad terms, with feeling. I want... _____

Bonus Points: Write out your eulogy and post it somewhere you'll see it every day.

If you think you are too small to make a difference,
try sleeping with a mosquito.
Dalai Lama

Chapter Eight

THE MOVE MINDSET: *BE A DUCK*

Please don't go, we'll eat you up we love you so!
Where The Wild Things Are by Maurice Sendak

My parents met in a psychology class at Cal State Long Beach in 1969. They were *both* psychology majors. As far back as I can remember, I wanted to be a psychologist with a Ph.D. and help people feel better about their lives. I attended a small college, majored in psychology, and loved it. I wanted to continue on to my Ph.D. However, I worried about the cost of more school. I worried about the time it would take. I worried I wasn't smart enough. I worried myself right into the ground. Then, I got stuck.

Three months after college graduation, I found a job as an assistant making $10 an hour at a manufacturing plant in Ontario, California. I attended graduate school at night. You're assuming in the psychology department, right? Nope. Business. To this day, I cannot explain why. I had zero interest in business. Before I could start the 12 courses required for the program, I had to take 13 prerequisite courses. Yes, thirteen. I spent the next five and a half years on that degree while working full-time and trying to keep my first marriage afloat (that's a whole other story). *Dang, there's so much I need to tell you!*

The manufacturing plant was even more glamorous. I was 21, wearing nylons and heels every day in a sawmill. My job required me to coordinate between the owner and all the department heads. These guys were twice my age, and I had no idea what I was doing. The first week left me in tears on the bathroom floor after my new boss berated me over the phone. No one had ever spoken to me like that before. I completely shut down. But, it wasn't just me. The bosses yelled at everyone. *What the heck? Is this what happens in the real world?* That was a major turning point for me. I pulled myself off the floor, blew my nose, and made a decision.

I would not begin my adult life as a victim. No way.

The next morning, I walked into my boss' office with a long note I'd written. I logically and confidently presented the facts and requested if he'd like me to do something differently, merely mentioning it will give him the results he'd like. If he screamed and cursed, he'd only have a weepy girl hiding in a bathroom. I had tears in my eyes as I read him my note. I was embarrassed. But, I got through it.

This could have backfired. I didn't know how he would respond. What I learned though was if you approach someone genuinely and honestly, your odds of a positive response go way up. In this case, it worked. He treated me with kindness and respect for the next three years. During those years, I learned how to talk to people from a wide variety of backgrounds. I learned about myself. Like how *not* to run meetings with men twice my age. I also learned more about business than in all 25 of my MBA courses combined.

Can you think of an instance where you missed an opportunity because you did not take action? A time in your life when you let go of a dream? What if you hadn't stopped pursuing it? What might your life look like now?

In the MOVE Mindset, you know what you want, but you might not know *how* to make it happen. Maybe you're too worried or maybe you don't have the time, resources, or energy to do it. This can be incredibly frustrating. The key is finding the right tools and tactics for *you,* at this point in your life, the ones that best fit your personality. Your lifestyle. Your values. You know yourself best.

The focus here: ACTION.

Nothing will ever be attempted if all possible objections must first be overcome.
Samuel Johnson

Be A Duck

When a mother duck wants to walk across the road for a swim in the pond, she doesn't wait calmly until her ducklings all get into a perfect line. Nor does she quack at them until they line up. She turns away from them, faces the direction she needs to go, and starts waddling. Guess what happens. *Yep.* The ducklings scurry into a line and follow her across the road.

The same goes for taking action on important life decisions. If you wait until everything magically aligns BEFORE you start waddling, you may wait forever.

It is difficult to steer a parked car, so get moving.
Henrietta Mears

Quick Happy Tips

In case there's a tornado headed your way (either real or figurative), here are four quick tips to help you feel calm, centered, and release an extra dose of feel-good oxytocin and serotonin into your brain:

1. **Listen to Music.** Not just *any* music, specifically, music from your teenage years. Or from a happy time in your life. Take ten minutes, make a channel on Pandora, download songs on iTunes, or go to the record shop for some albums.
2. **Start Moving.** Skip around, dance, do yoga, or pretend you know karate. Anything that makes you smile and gets your heart rate up for 5 to 10 minutes. Your kids will think it's hilarious, unless they are teenagers. Then, they may roll their eyes and text their friends a video of their crazy mom.
3. **See Nature.** Watch trees blowing in the breeze, birds flying around in the sky, waves rolling in the ocean – anything not made by humans. Oh, and try to breathe. Use your eyeballs to look and use your lungs to breathe, *almost like you're a real human being.*
4. **Feel Nature.** Walk barefoot in the grass. Watch the trees sway in the breeze. Or, feel the warm sun your face.

Now, if the tornado has passed, we can focus on what you really want. First things first. *You need more time, right?*

How to Make Time

What is the simplest way to make more time in your life?

Stop doing other stuff. One of my favorite tips is from billionaire and life coach Jon Butcher. His *Stop Doing List* is the simplest way to make more time for yourself. Make a list of the top five things you do every day that waste a bunch of your time. Come on, you already know them: stuff like Facebook, Instagram, talking to people you don't even like very much, Netflix, eating food when you're not even hungry, etc. *It can be a mental list.*

Most of the time, these are also the things that bring resentment, anger, anxiety or frustration into your life. If watching a sitcom on Netflix before bed is your happy time, then keep it. However, if you spend hours going down the toilet drain of political news, celebrity scandal, or stalking old friends on FB - then stand up, say your name, and admit you have a problem.

Try testing your addiction by trying to abstain for three days. No, vacations and work conventions don't count. Do it when your schedule is as typical as can be.

How much time would that free up? A couple of minutes? A few hours? Is your mood lighter? Do you have more patience with the people you'd like to keep in your life?

My Stop It List:

I replaced listening to talk radio or music in my car with listening to audio books.

I replaced manicures with a $20 day pass at a Korean spa.

I replaced watching Netflix before bed with meditating.

I replaced reading the news each morning with doing a 4-7 minute zero-sweat workout.

Seriously, this Stop It List freed up A LOT of time, time I never realized I had. The year I began working on this book, I read over 50 books. All of these Stop Doing choices also made me happier and healthier. I felt more patient, more relaxed, and more optimistic about my future.

When I made the above changes, I was shocked how much I didn't miss the radio, the E! Channel, or news radio *at all*. It was amazing how much more I focused on what I *wanted* in my life. I stopped feeling whisked away by the current of all the chaos around me. I visited the hotel gym last week, turned on the TV and was surprised to find every channel filled with gruesome news stories, violent crime dramas, or junk reality shows.

I was so accustomed to it before. I never noticed how negative and superficial it all was. I also didn't realize how pessimistic it made me feel about humanity, the planet, and the future. I feel so much better after eliminating these time-sucking and brain-numbing habits. Now, I can spend my limited time and energy on the activities and the projects and the people that are important to me and make me feel happy.

Knowing is not enough; we must apply.
Being willing is not enough; we must do.
Leonardo da Vinci

Stop It List

I highly suggest adding to this list any activities that leave you feeling upset or anxious. For instance, that friend you love but who is always super angry or depressed? Minimize that type of interaction as much as possible. Send a quick email to touch base and give support. That's it. You don't have to be held hostage by their emotional quicksand. If you find yourself surrounded by coworkers, friends, or family members like this, notice it. Take a breath. Get some distance from them. Then, keep an eye out for people who are kind, inspiring, and happy.

The more time you spend with these positive people, the better you will feel too. Often, the perpetually unhappy folks will realize you're no longer feeding into their negativity. They probably won't like it. If you're lucky, your positivity and enthusiasm will either inspire them or cause them to avoid you completely.

The 80/20 Principle

This rule states 80% of the results we get in our life stem from 20% of our efforts. For instance, 20% of your clients might lead to 80% of your profits. Similarly, 20% of your friends and family create 80% of the stress or anxiety in your life. (In the next chapter we will talk about the *Let It Be* attitude, to help deal with the problem people in your life who are impossible to avoid.)

If you can identify the one out of five people who cause you the most heartache or irritation, then you can rethink the time you spend with those not positively contributing to your life. If you uncover which 20 of your 100 customers bring you the most business, then you know where to spend most of your time and energy.

Spend **most** of your energy and time and money on the 20% of your life that brings you the **most benefits**. Then, the remaining tasks and activities can be delegated, ignored, hired out, or delayed. Similarly, once you identify the 20% of the activities and people who cause you the **most frustration,** you can eliminate them. *Just kidding.* Please don't eliminate anybody. Instead, you can minimize the time and energy you spend with those 20% problem people and problem environments.

Get Moving Tricks

Parkinson's Law

This is the law of deadlines. When you have a goal with a deadline that is weeks or months away, it's likely to appear more daunting and more complex than a goal with a tight deadline.

You will be more effective and efficient when you have a short amount of time to complete a task. You don't have time to screw around, distract yourself, or make excuses.

How to use this tool: Set concrete deadlines for your goals (or pieces of a larger goal) LESS THAN the amount of time you think you need. For example, if you need to send your resume to five companies in the next week, make your due date today! If you want to finish writing chapter six by the end of the month, give yourself one week. If you want to research a new job opportunity, take ten minutes right now to set up an appointment with someone who can help guide you. Then, meet them within the week, if at all possible.

Psychologically, when we know we have time to do something, a million distractions and interruptions crop up to block us. Have you ever noticed when an emergency happens, everything else becomes unimportant? What if your child gets a concussion and cannot remember where he is (which happened to me last Friday afternoon)? There's nothing like a trip to the ER in Nashville, TN to help you shuffle unimportant stuff to the bottom of the deck. *Don't wait for an emergency to put your priorities in order, my friend.*

MicroGoals

Setting MicroGoals is an ingenious trick to get you moving. When faced with a daunting goal, you might lack the confidence to begin, the persistence to continue, or the self-control to keep distractions at bay. MicroGoals can help you conquer all three of these obstacles. Here are three secrets to setting a great MicroGoal:

1. Make it so incredibly **TINY**, it's too embarrassing NOT to do it! For example, *Today I will complete ONE sit-up.* You will likely end up doing at least a few more.

Either way, this builds confidence and forces you to start moving in the right direction.

2. Make sure it's **TIED** to a larger goal. Linking the goal to one of your Top Five will make you a healthier, happier human. If I set a MicroGoal to boil one egg, but I despise cooking and find no value in it, then it's not the right micro-goal for me. *Hmm, maybe my goal should be minimizing or delegating my cooking responsibilities?* If I've always wanted to learn to cook, yet never find the time, then I'm on the right track.

3. Do it at the right **TIME** for *you.* For me, this time would be after my morning coffee, but before anything else. *Maybe your time is after taking the dog for her walk, or right before dinner, or after everyone else is asleep and the kitchen is clean.*

Gamify It

MindValley founder and author, Vishen Lakhiani, tells a simple story about Gamification. He gamified his start-up business. His website sold meditation videos. It started small. If he sold enough videos to buy himself a Starbucks coffee each morning, he celebrated! When he succeeded in winning his free coffee for a couple of weeks, he upped his goal to coffee AND a Subway sandwich for lunch.

Instead of becoming discouraged about his measly $10 per day profit, he reveled in the fact he got a free coffee and a free lunch every day. Vishen continued to up his game every month. He started with a $700 investment. It didn't happen overnight, but gamifying his goals made it far more fun and rewarding during those difficult beginning years. His business, MindValley, is now valued at $40 million dollars, only 16 years later.

What can you gamify? Maybe your goal requires some not-so-fun work. *That's the part you gamify.* Need to scan through miles of boring data to find potential investors? For every ten investors you find, you get a phone call to your best friend, a bubble bath, or a hunk of that chocolate bar from the freezer.

High Performer Tricks

Psychologist and motivational speaker Marisa Peer recommends you copy what high performers do naturally. Marisa reports extremely happy people who are also successful share four core traits:

1. They are willing to do what they hate to get what they want. *Don't be afraid of digging in the dirt to find your golden nugget.*
2. They are great at delaying gratification. *Do your least-favorite work first.*
3. They are excellent at bouncing back from their failures and mistakes. *Don't let setbacks prevent you from continuing forward.*
4. They take one step toward their goals every single day. They do not take a break: not for a birthday, a vacation, or an illness. *Do something every day that moves you toward your ultimate end goal.*

Creating Your Goals

Even the best tools and tricks on the planet will only work when they are *right* for you, when they fit your personality and your life. A 5 a.m. group workout class? *No way!*

Take an online class? *Not for me!*

When it comes to finding the right tools, you must consider your personality, values, and current lifestyle. For instance, I'm a morning person, I love checking stuff off lists, and I hate doing the same things every day. So, writing at night and keeping the same schedule each day, doesn't work for me. It feels forced, hard, and I know I won't keep up with it.

If I have a goal or a change I'm trying to make in my life, it helps me most to relate it to a bigger goal down the road (yes, my Top Five). I also remove the guilt by reminding myself I'm modeling good self-care to my kids. I want to show them not only is failure OK, but it allows me to learn a lot. I also want them to see *not trying* is far worse than failing. Then, I create some MicroGoals and start visualizing my future, as if I've already succeeded. For instance, every night I envision this book helping hundreds of thousands of women. I see the completed book in my hands, with a big best-selling sticker plastered on the cover! I see emails filling my inbox from women telling me how their lives have changed as a result of reading this book.

Let's figure out what will work best for *you* now. I know I said these assignments are optional, *but please don't skip this one!*

MINI-HOMEWORK ASSIGNMENT (6 minutes)

The MOVE Personality Test

1. What is your most productive time of day?
2. Do you work best with a team, a partner, or alone?
3. Who can you share this goal with for support, encouragement, and accountability?

Choose ONE of the following tools laid out in this chapter and try it. Today.

☐ Create Your *Stop It* List
☐ 80/20 Analysis

- [ ] Parkinson's Law
- [ ] MicroGoals
- [ ] Gamify It
- [ ] High Performer Tricks

If you wait long enough to make dinner,
everyone will just eat cereal. It's science.
@sarcasticmommy4

Chapter Nine

THE BELIEVE MINDSET: *YOUR BALONEY BELIEFS*

The moment you doubt whether you can fly,
you cease forever to be able to do it.
Peter Pan by J.M. Barrie

On the first day of my college art class, the professor asked us to paint a picture of our classmates' faces. This was "Painting Fundamentals." I thought the first assignment might be how to make shades of green from blue and yellow. Clearly, she wanted to weed out the real artists from us wannabes. My painting was awful. Really terrible. It looked like something your six-year-old might draw while blindfolded, after a dose of Benadryl. She winced at my painting and said, *did you LOOK at his face?* Rude! I muddled my way through the class and she reluctantly gave me a B-. *I was not happy.*

Twelve years passed before I picked up another paintbrush. I was, at the time, thoroughly depressed about not being able to get pregnant. Every month I'd obsess, exhausted and drained from the emotional roller coaster. Up, up I'd go with fantasies of a positive test and all that would mean for the next months and years of my life. Then, I'd fall down, down, down into a pit of despair when the test strip revealed just one line. No matter how hard I looked. No matter what light I held it up to. No matter how hard I squinted at it or how I turned it sideways up against the mirror. *Ha, ha, ha,* says the universe. *You're not pregnant! Again!*

Docs said, "Don't worry. We'll just knock you out and remove your fallopian tubes. Then, we'll do in vitro." Have I mentioned I'm terrible with needles? My heart races. I spew sweat. My adrenaline spikes. My eyeballs roll back in my head. Then, I pass out. *Literally.* Jaimie once caught me from falling to the floor as I passed out during a routine blood test. Needles make me super nervous. My *Monkey Gut* assured me my anxiety would prevent any successful in vitro procedure. Adoption would be our answer if I couldn't get pregnant the old-fashioned-style.

At that dark point in my life, I turned to art. I needed a release for all the pent-up frustration and sadness I felt. I bought three big blank, white canvases. I used a lot of red paint. Black too. I slathered paint all over those blank boards. It felt incredible. The paint was thick and gloppy. I didn't bother to water it down at all. It felt good to give the canvases some depth and texture. I didn't know you were *supposed* to add water to the paint. It felt so good; I continued painting even after I eventually got pregnant.

Here's what happened: I started acupuncture, and began the adoption process for a baby in China. After six months of paperwork, social worker meetings, and translation documents,

I found out I was pregnant. I was shocked. You see, I was fairly certain no second line existed on those test strips. I'd looked and stared at so many of them. I'd pee on the strips several days before they could possibly come up with an accurate answer. I'd do it several times a day for four or five days each month. By my estimations, I used more than 227 strips.

Before you feel too sorry for me, I have to admit my struggle to conceive lasted not for eight years, or five years, or even three years, like so many women I know. No. It was about 18 months. *I know, I know! It's embarrassing.* I hereby apologize to you if you waited longer, or you're still waiting now. *I'm so sorry I was obnoxiously impatient!*

Ok, back to my point about the art class and my rude professor. *Did you look at his face?* One little comment from someone I barely knew prevented me from painting for over a decade. I internalized her words. I believed her. *I was not an artist.* Luckily, I hit a level of sadness that was so profound, it overpowered that belief. I didn't care; I would paint anyway. Screw her.

I kept painting. After a couple of years, I started receiving some positive feedback. I scheduled a few art shows. I painted large, abstract acrylic pieces. Three years, two babies, and a five art shows later, I'd sold about $20,000 in paintings. I only wish it hadn't taken 12 years and a deep depression to challenge my mistaken belief.

Never let anyone tell you you're not an artist.

You can have anything you want if you are willing to give up the belief that you can't have it.
Robert Anthony, Ph.D.

Basic Beliefs and Baloney Beliefs

Sometimes knowing what you want, having all the best tools, and using them diligently, is not enough to break through the negative beliefs you hold about yourself. In the ASK chapter, you identified what you want. In the MOVE chapter, you learned tools and tricks to make it happen. But sadly, those are often not enough. *That's why this book doesn't end here Missy.*

We all have basic, core beliefs we carry with us every day. Beliefs about ourselves, our role in the family, how much money we should earn, and what type of life we should be living. Your beliefs guide you through life. Right now you could probably list your core beliefs if someone asked you. Maybe you believe in being honest, working hard, and loving your family unconditionally. However, these are not the beliefs I am talking about. I'm talking about the ones you don't even realize are there, just below your conscious awareness.

These are beliefs you have carried with you for years and years and never even questioned. Stuff like:

I'm terrible with directions.

I'll never make enough money to retire young.

I'll always be overweight, no matter what I do.

These are *Baloney Beliefs*. Some might be super helpful; others are hazardous. Either way, if you don't know they're messing with you, *how can you decide which ones you want to keep?*

Your Poop Mole

Baloney Beliefs are even sneakier than your little bird, Rebecca. Instead of chirping at you, they are incredibly quiet. They're like that little mole on your shoulder. It's been there so long, you don't notice it anymore. It's just become part of who you are. Except, once you look closely, you realize it's not a mole at all. Nope. It's poop. A tiny speck of dried poop. Not only is it *not* helping you, it's making your life quite *stinky*. Once you realize it's fecal matter and not a mole, it's simple to get a tissue and wipe it away. *Maybe also take a shower.*

Baloney Beliefs are just like poop moles. Once you realize they are not helpful to your life, you can decide to wipe them away. These are actually much easier to eliminate than *iShoulds* because they lose much of their power once they reach your conscious level.

Finding Your Poop Moles

Uncovering a *Baloney Belief* is the tricky part. They are subtle and sneaky. *Pssst. Hey there Mama, you're not supposed to make more money than your husband!* They speak to us when we're watching a soccer game, making dinner, filing our taxes, or cleaning out the lint trap in the dryer.

What beliefs do you carry around subconsciously? What *Baloney Beliefs* are spoiling your plans for happiness? Where did they come from? How do you root them out of their hiding places and make them stand in front of the class? Only then you can decide for yourself, with your conscious, adult, awesome brain; *do I truly believe this?*

Where Do They Come From?

Often, you pick up your *Baloney Beliefs* as a child. *Money is scarce, and those who have lots of it are greedy and unkind.* In other instances, the *Baloney Belief* comes from your culture, your society, or your religion. What lurking beliefs do you have about women, being a parent, having money? What function should food serve? What does a good boss do? What kind of job are you supposed to have? What are you supposed to do during the holidays?

These subconscious beliefs are not always negative. You could have a dream-squashing belief in one area of your life and a dream-fueling belief in another area. For instance, maybe you believe you can find any job you want and will always be well paid. But in your relationships, you believe people are untrustworthy and will always disappoint you.

Pssst. Wealthy people are mean and greedy, right?

Pssst. You are resilient and can survive anything!

Pssst. You'll never be in a healthy and happy relationship, so just stay where you are.

The question is this: Which of these beliefs are helpful to you, and which are not? Is it a beauty mark or a poop mole?

Step One: Uncover a *Baloney Belief.*

Step Two: Decide if you want to keep it

We must believe we are gifted for something, and that this thing, at whatever cost, must be attained.

Marie Curie

Joe's Baloney Money Belief

Author Joe Vitale tells a great story about his father. For years, Joe had never earned over $250,000. This is a whole lot of money for most of us. The amount is not the point. For Joe, it made no sense why he could never seem to break through this magical number. Until, one day after a meditation session, he realized $250,000 was the exact amount his father had earned at the height of his career. Somehow, Joe created a *Baloney Belief* that it was disrespectful to earn more money than his father had earned.

After talking together, Joe realized his father would be proud if Joe could surpass all of his successes. The following year, Joe easily broke through the magical number. He smashed his *Baloney Belief* merely by bringing it out into the open.

Now It's Your Turn

If you had a job you loved, perfect health, and made enough money to do anything you wanted, what *Baloney Belief* would you have to toss out first? What belief might be secretly sabotaging you while you're busy working your tail off?

Maybe part of you fears what might happen when this belief is no longer holding you back? It's not always black and white. There are pros and cons to everything. Sometimes, there are dang good reasons NOT to achieve your dreams and goals. *I'm serious, my friend.*

Examples:

* *If finally, after all these years I move past this block, it means I suffered all that time for nothing? No way, I cannot stand that thought!*
* *If I get into amazing shape, men might approach me more, which makes me super uncomfortable.*
* *If I had my own company, I might have to travel and be away from my children. I am not ready for that!*

The Baloney Beliefs Quiz

Let's try uncovering some of your *Baloney Beliefs*.
Fill in the following blanks:

1. Making over _____ dollars a year will never happen for me. (40,000? 250,000? 4 Million!?)
2. Weighing _____ lbs will never be a reality for me.
3. Having a career where I can _____ is just impossible for me right now. (Work part time? Work from home? Travel more? Travel less?)

4. Having a partner who treats me like
_____ is never gonna happen.
5. Spending two weeks in _____ with
_____ doing _____
is only a fantasy.

My Story: I Deserve This

A few years ago I saw a show called "Million Dollar Listing." These 20-year-old boys were making TWO MILLION dollars a year! They did not appear to be particularly smart or magically handsome. In my opinion, they were obnoxious. Why should they make that kind of money? I immediately thought: *I'm smarter and nicer than them. I definitely work harder. I would do much better things with that money than go to clubs and buy $400 loafers.* At that very moment, something clicked in my brain.

My financial glass ceiling shattered.

I felt freed. Freed from a belief I didn't even realize I had. My Baloney Belief: *If I earned "too much" money, it would be obnoxious and not fair to those around me whom I loved and respected.*

These are the sort of beliefs that stop us from realizing so many of our dreams. Often, just by bringing these beliefs into the light, they wither up and die. Think of someone who has what you want in one life area. Are they smarter than you? More attractive? Have more resources? *What do you have that they do not?*

Who are your obnoxious-millionaire-realtors?

Your neighbors? A coworker? Your cousin Ross? (Maybe I've watched too many episodes of *Friends*.)

Ask yourself: *Why not me?*

Squashing Your *Baloney Beliefs*

How do we unravel these beliefs? How do we starve them so they lose their power over us?

Ask yourself:

1. Do I truly believe this now, as an adult? If your answer is no, then your work here is done.
2. When did this belief come into my life? Who planted it? What did I experience that buried it so deeply into my subconscious?
3. What might my life have been like if I never carried this belief? What choices would I have made differently?

Mini-Homework: Making A Replacement Belief

Once you've identified your *Baloney Beliefs*, how do you establish a healthier belief in its place? Here are some tools to try out: (pick one)

1. Write it out. Do a free-write in your journal. Just let go and write and write without overthinking. Often, you'll know you're getting somewhere if you feel emotional. When the tears well up in your eyes, you know you've hit on something important. Then, write out what you want to believe about yourself instead.
2. Use your Top Five to link your new belief to the traits and qualities most important to you.
3. Make a mental or written list of all the ways having this new belief will benefit those around you. What would it mean for your partner, your children, your coworkers? If you believed this healthier option, who else might benefit? Maybe you'd be happier and less stressed. I'm guessing *lots* of people around you would appreciate that!

4. Think about what you might experience if you replaced your *Baloney Belief* with something more helpful to you. What new opportunities might you act upon? What new possibilities might be open to you?

My fake plants died because I did not
pretend to water them.
Mitch Hedberg

Chapter Ten

THE ELEVATE MINDSET: *LET IT BE*

> *I don't understand it any more than you do,*
> *but one thing I've learned is that you don't have to*
> *understand things for them to be.*
> **A Wrinkle in Time by Madeleine L'Engle**

was in 100% *reactive mode*. I spent all day responding to the needs, wants, and minor emergencies of everyone around me. Like a catcher in a baseball game. Except, balls flew at me from all directions. Some were ping-pong balls. Others were bowling balls. Some had spikes. Others were covered in syrup. All day long, frantically, catching and throwing. *Sound familiar?* I'd collapse at the end of the day, exhausted, but not quite sure what I'd accomplished.

 Exhaustion without a sense of accomplishment = Frustration and Resentment

In 2016, I turned 42 and started meditating. Mostly, I breathed slowly with my eyes closed. I'd do it first thing in the morning and last thing before bed at night. At first, my brain bounced around like a six-year-old in a jumpy castle. It got easier, and the benefits became more obvious as the weeks rolled by. Eventually, random answers or solutions to things I'd been thinking about would suddenly pop into my head. I kept a pad and paper nearby. I'd stop, jot down my little epiphanies, then try to get back into *the zone*.

The important thing I want to share with you is what I noticed right away.

I was calmer. I slept better. I had more patience with myself, with my children, and with my husband. I felt like my days were more *on purpose*. I felt more in control of where I placed my time and energy throughout the day. *My inner control freak was much happier.* As they say in Transcendental Meditation, I started *responding* instead of *reacting* to the people and events in my life.

The Elevate Mindset is about learning how to control your emotional reactivity so you can better tolerate the physical and emotional demands of your life. Want to hear the secret recipe for feeling calmer, more focused, and less frazzled? Oh, it'll also help you look better, feel better, and sleep better! *Ready for it?*

It's science.

There are a few specific hormones and chemicals that are closely linked to your emotional states. When these chemicals are released for too long or in elevated amounts, it's bad news for you both physically and emotionally. I'm talking about cortisol and adrenaline. *I know you don't need a science lecture right now.* I promise to keep it simple.

Cortisol and adrenaline are important because they impact your sleep (*remember how awesome sleep was?*), your metabolism (*remember your waistline?*), your emotional reactivity (*remember when you were patient?*), and even your wrinkles (*I mean you look amazing, but let's keep you that way*).

The Stress Hormone

Cortisol. The more often you feel stressed, panicked, or anxious, the more cortisol your body produces. This is life-saving if you're about to get hit by a car or chased by a masked bandit. Cortisol increases your blood sugar and your blood pressure. It slows down your immune system, your digestion, and your reproductive drive, so you can focus on survival.

We're late for school again! The garbage disposal broke! I can't find my cell phone! I know you have many reasons to feel agitated and anxious. But, these events are not life-threatening. *Irritating?* Yes. *Frustrating?* Definitely. But, your life is not *literally* in danger.

Unfortunately, your Neanderthal brain doesn't know the difference. None of those problems require a racing heart or a slower metabolism. They don't need a liter of blood to rush down from your brain and out to your muscles. A slower metabolism won't help you stay calm and focused during your big presentation. A racing heart won't help you remember you left your cell phone on the edge of the sink.

Every little stressful experience tells your brain to *release more cortisol.* These prolonged, elevated levels of cortisol can lead to anxiety, depression, digestive problems, headaches, sleep issues, weight gain, and difficulties with memory and concentration.[1] *As if we don't have enough problems already!*

The Fight or Flight Hormone

Adrenaline. When your brain believes you're in danger, it releases additional adrenaline to help you out. This increases your heart rate, gets you breathing faster, and sends lots of good blood to your muscles. *Perfect, if you're about to arm wrestle the manager at Ikea.*

Like cortisol, adrenaline is not so helpful unless you're in physical danger. Maybe you're late because you cannot find your car keys? You're stressed. Flustered. *You just had them in your hand a minute ago!* Your brain isn't working right because your body thinks you're about to fight a rhino. Not only is this *not* helpful, but too much adrenaline can give you a weakened immune system, insomnia, peptic ulcers, anxiety, and even depression.[2]

If you ever need to lift a car off your toddler, *bring on the adrenaline!* Otherwise, it's best for your brain to remain calm and cool. *So, how do you better manage your cortisol and adrenaline levels?*

Let's start simple.

Breathe, Chew, Drink, and Eat

There are a few secrets I've found helpful in situations where I need my brain (*so I can focus*), my patience (*so I don't scream at strangers in the market*), and my body (*so I don't feel fatigued and exhausted by 2 p.m. every day*) to function properly.

Breathe Deeply

Breathing gets oxygen into your cells and removes carbon dioxide and other toxins from your tissues. Slow, deep breathing also reduces your heart rate and blood pressure. It gives you a healthy balance of oxygen and carbon dioxide in your blood. Deep breathing increases your ability to concentrate, focus, and think more clearly.[3] *Ahh, wouldn't that be nice?* The first step to controlling your cortisol and adrenaline is taking slow, deep breaths. Coincidentally, the first step to meditation is also taking slow, deep breaths. Breathe. The next time you feel your anxiety or frustration levels rise, breathe as slowly and deeply as possible, *for as long as you can stand it.*

Chew Gum

Chewing on gum makes your brain think you're eating. If you're eating, your Neanderthal brain assumes you must *not* be in a life-threatening situation. *You're safe.* Chewing fools your brain into thinking you are calm and cool as a cucumber. Cortisol levels decrease, mental alertness increases, and the anxious chatter quiets.[4] *Easy, right?*

Feed Your Body

There are 80 million books and websites about how and what you *should* eat. But, that's not why you're reading this book. *Or, you're going to be disappointed.* This book exists to give you tips and inspiration to feel calmer, happier, and mentally healthier as a human. I'm not saying stop drinking, starve yourself, or eliminate chocolate. *I would never say that about chocolate.* But, more and more studies show food is as effective as drugs. Food can impact you in fantastic ways or in awful ways.

You know yourself best. For instance, I know if I drink too much wine, I get headaches and cannot sleep. *Tito's Vodka with soda water and a splash of cranberry is my current drink of choice.* If I eat cereal with milk first thing in the morning, I feel sick to my stomach. If I forget to drink water regularly, my head starts pounding by 3 p.m.

We all have different genetics, cravings, and allergies. If you pay attention, you can tell which foods make you feel crummy, and which make you feel amazing. *You know* when you've eaten too much or not eaten enough. *You know* when your body might need a lower dosage of alcohol or sugar or coffee or when your body needs more greens and veggies. *You know* water is good for you and, *you know* too much of anything is bad news.

Notice what you're eating... *How do you feel?*

breathe

If you eat a bit more of the healthier foods and a bit less of the richer, sweeter, or fattier foods, you might sleep better, feel better, and even look better. Again, this is about *you*. What will make *you* feel better every day and, better for the next seventy years?

Oh, your mother thinks you're overweight? Your partner thinks you should take more vitamins? You are responsible for your own health. *You* are the boss of your own body. *You.*

It's easy to get hung up on calories or the number of pounds displayed on that annoying electric scale. It's easy to feel resentful or discouraged when you see pictures of yourself from years and years ago. But, why beat yourself up? *What is the point?* Try this, notice what you're eating and drinking. *Think balance.* Notice how your body feels. Most importantly, be nice to yourself. Try speaking to yourself as you would speak to a friend. Even better; if you wouldn't say it aloud to someone you just met, don't say it to yourself. *That's reasonable, right?*

My current health-related mantra: *I'm so grateful I eat and drink and move in a way that's healthiest for my body.*

Move Your Body

Moving is good for your body. Sitting on the sofa all day or staring at a computer screen for 12 hours is *not ideal.* Moving is good for you physically and mentally. Now we know it's also good for you emotionally. Exercise allows your body to practice its stress response, increasing communication between your central nervous system, your cardiovascular system, and your muscles. This helps you develop a healthier response to mental stressors. The more you practice *physically* stressing your body, the better you get at remaining calm during *emotional* and *psychological* stressors.

Moving your body releases the *feel-good* chemicals in your brain, called endorphins. The more sedentary we are, the less efficiently our bodies respond to stressful events and experiences.[5] Almost any form of exercise can act as a stress reliever. You hate running, but you love rock climbing? You hate tennis, but you love swimming? Do whatever you enjoy at this point in your life. Or, whatever you hate the least.

For example, I've found I like to switch up my exercise regimen every three months. I like to swim in the ocean or a lake, but not a pool. I like to dance and do yoga, but I hate running. I'm pretty terrible at any sport that requires balls, but

I like hikes and walks. Find what works for you and your body. You're more likely to do it and you just might find you love it.

Let It Be, Forgive, and Feel Grateful

One of the reasons I don't practice as a Marriage and Family Therapist anymore is while I *really* like to be helpful, I also *really* like to control stuff. *I will help you whether you like it or not!* I used to think about my clients' problems all the time. Constantly. I'd imagine what they could say or do that might ease their emotional pain. I didn't have the patience to allow them to heal at their own pace. I'd get frustrated. I couldn't understand why clients wouldn't follow through on their plans or why they kept sabotaging themselves. *If you'd just do this, right now, your life would be SO much better!* Finally, I realized it's not that simple. It's not very helpful either.

This is *not* a new problem for me. I was always a bossy little thing. Even in kindergarten, my childhood friend George had to be separated from me and placed in another classroom. Apparently, I bossed him around all the time. *Sorry about that, George!* In high school, I thought it was my job to get everyone on time to cheerleading practice. *Yes, I admit it. I was a cheerleader.* But, I wasn't one of those annoying ones.

I'm lying. I was *so* annoying. I even annoyed the other cheerleaders. I'd drive around picking everyone up if they couldn't get to practice on time. I was appalled when nobody agreed to choreograph a new routine for our senior year performance. They just wanted to do the same old routine so they could spend their free time enjoying their last year of high school. *What kind of crazy thinking is that?* I was a total pain in their *adolescence*. Of course, I finally realized this about myself (a few months ago). I am much better now. I'm learning how to *Let It Be*, which helps tremendously.

Let It Be

This, my friend, is the golden key to reducing the excess stress in your life. *Let it be.* It means to let go. It means not spending your time and energy trying to control or change others. It means releasing your expectations. Yes, people change. But, it's rarely because you *want* them to change. Or, because you *need* them to change. Or, because you think they *ought* to change.

Believe it or not, you're not on Earth to get everyone to believe the same as you, think the same as you, or act the same as you. Oh, and it's also not your job to save anyone from themselves. Maybe you don't have this problem. Feel free to skip ahead if it's just me. Otherwise, pay attention because this concept will save you heaps of frustration. Either way, there's a big difference between helping others because *they* want to be helped and helping others because *you* want them to be helped.

What do you do?

1. Let go of your judgments towards others. *Judgments about their thoughts, words, and actions.*
2. Let go of trying to control others. *Controlling their thoughts, words, and actions.*

3. Let go of feeling offended by others. *Offended by their…
   Yeah, you got it.*
4. Let go of the judgments you carry toward yourself.

I know, this is hard. But, I promise, it's worth it. When you're able to *Let It Be*, you let go of judgement towards others. You let go of judgments towards yourself. You let go of what you *wish* had happened. You accept what IS.

breathe

What helps me *Let It Be*:

1. Repeat daily: *I'm so thankful I allow others to act and speak with acceptance, love, and understanding.*
2. I remind myself we are all on our own little journey and, we all have various lessons we will learn *or not learn,* along the way. I'm not in any position to judge the words or actions of others. Yeah, I'll protect my children from danger and unhealthy environments whenever possible. I'll remove myself from unhealthy relationships and situations as well. But, I will not waste my time or energy judging others.

To Let It Be means you're not fighting it. You're not trying to control it. You're not even upset about it. Think about that for a moment. What if you were truly able to *Let It Go* when someone hurt your feelings, when you made a mistake, or when a situation did not go as planned? *Argh, that jerk just cut me off and now I missed the light! That receptionist was so rude to me! I cannot believe Erica's mother just completely ignored me!*

Life appears to me to be too short to be spent in nursing animosity or registering wrongs.
Charlotte Bronte

Forgiveness

If you read a lot of personal development books, you already know gratitude plays a critical role in your mental health. Well, forgiveness is the new gratitude. Studies now show forgiving past wrongs is even more beneficial than feeling thankful. Forgiveness is intertwined with the *Let It Be* approach. They are the same basic concept but with a twist. When you forgive someone, you hop inside your mental time machine and go back to the initial moment of insult. Then, you *Let It Be*. You accept others and their actions with as little negative emotion and judgement as you can muster.

An important point about forgiveness came up in a Stretch Marks Retreat: What if the person you're trying to forgive is currently part of your life? What if this person actively causes you emotional or physical injury? First, start the forgiveness practice with someone who is in your past, and no longer hurting you. Second, learn to set up emotionally-protective boundaries when dealing with painful people in your life. *This is far easier said than done, I know.*

Baby steps. Start with this: You are worthy of protection from hurtful people. **You are worthy of love. You are worthy of respect. You are worthy of receiving kindness and love.** If you were told repeatedly by caregivers you were not worthy, please begin the reverse-brainwash process immediately.

Every morning, repeat to yourself the bolded words above. Brainwash yourself back to a healthier state of mind. Your loved ones will appreciate and see a difference too.

breathe

If, at the time of the emotional injury, you were truly allowing and accepting of the situation or person involved, you would not have had any resentment, jealousy, or pain to carry with you into the future. *Does that make sense?* So, to forgive is like going back in time to allow that person to be and do, without judgment. If you want to let go of past resentments, start with forgiving people who caused you a *minor* irritation or pain. Then, slowly work your way up to the big stuff.

Who do you forgive?
1. People you've been angry with for so long it's become comfortable.
2. People you're angry with out of principle. *It's just not right! They don't deserve my forgiveness!*
3. People you think you've forgiven, but not so much. Journaling or doing a free-write will help uncover these folks. *If you find tears welling up or strong emotions as you write, it means you have some emotional baggage you're dragging with you as you move through your life.*
4. Yourself.

Resentment is like drinking poison and then hoping it will kill your enemies.
Nelson Mandela

Be Grateful

Speaking of gratitude, I'll take a minute to remind you how much this practice can benefit your life. Feeling gratitude can reduce your cortisol levels, improve your immune system, and even help you live a longer life. Stop for a moment. Think of one thing you are grateful for. No, you cannot just say 'health' or 'family'. Be more specific. *I'm so grateful I have good friends I can trust and rely on.* Or, *I'm so grateful we have a pediatrician we love and who takes our insurance!* It can be big or small, as long as it's specific.

Refocusing your brain on something you feel grateful for will distract your Neanderthal brain. It also helps you to take a step back and gain perspective. Even if it's a problem you need to respond to immediately, it's still beneficial to take a broader look at the situation. *Yes, your kid is sick and just vomited all over the kitchen floor.* But, your neighbor will hang with your toddler while you take your six-year-old to the pediatrician. *How lucky are you?!*

By refocusing your attention on something positive, your cortisol and adrenaline levels can subside. Gratitude also increases dopamine, which is associated with pleasure and improves your quality of sleep.[6] Yes, you're tricking that Neanderthal brain of yours. *And, if doing it leaves you calmer, happier, and sleeping through the night, then game on!*

Always forgive your enemies;
nothing annoys them so much.
Oscar Wilde

Chapter Eleven

THE RADIATE MINDSET: *SELFISHLY GOOD*

'Why did you do all this for me?' he asked.
'I don't deserve it. I've never done anything for you.'
'You have been my friend,' replied Charlotte.
'That in itself is a tremendous thing.'
Charlotte's Web by E.B. White

I was at a hospital cafeteria a few weeks ago. The woman in front of me forgot her purse. She asked the cashier if she could leave her coffee while she left to retrieve it. I interrupted and said, *I've got it, please don't worry about getting your purse.* It cost me a whopping $1.40. She was surprised and grateful and offered to find me in our hospital room to repay me. *It's all good. You can pay for someone else's coffee next time you're here.* It was a tiny gesture. But it left her feeling good, me feeling good, and even the cashier had a big smile on his face.

Wanna feel extremely happy? Help other folks. Or help animals. Or help your town. Help anyone other than yourself and your immediate family. Helping others doesn't mean you have to start a charity to stop domestic violence. You don't have to quit your job to volunteer at the animal shelter 24/7, or donate your entire bank account to Alzheimer's research. *Though if you can and you want to, please go for it!* Helping others can be as simple as opening the door for someone, complimenting the receptionist on her smile, or taking a cup of coffee to your neighbor. Small gestures can set off a cascade of good feelings.

Kindness is contagious. How you feel inside, projects outward. Your facial expressions, your words, and your actions amplify your inner self. When you're happy and light on the inside, you can radiate that outward. When you act generously, those who benefit and those who witness it are more likely to act generously. Your brain releases dopamine when you do nice things for other people. This neurochemical acts as a little reward center and makes you feel happier and more optimistic. Researcher's call it the *helper's high*.

People who volunteer also report a decrease in chronic pain, lower blood pressure, and improved self-esteem. That day at the hospital, we all had a little *helper's high,* and I'll bet each one of us was more likely to make another gesture of kindness that day.

By the way, grouchiness is also contagious. You can choose to radiate kindness and joy, or you can radiate worry, fear, and frustration. Someone cuts you off on your way to work, you spill your coffee, you snap at a receptionist, he snaps at someone on the phone, and on and on. It can be tough to turn it around. When you see news reports about violent, angry, destructive events, it can affect your mood negatively.

Radiate the Good Stuff.

I always remember the story of a college student who became valedictorian of his class. In his speech, he tells how he and his best friend met in high school. The boy was a target of bullies and was extremely depressed. The friend noticed him walking home from high school one day, a heap of books in his arms. He introduced himself and offered a hand. They walked together and talked. They made plans to meet up the next day. Eventually, they became close friends and attended the same college.

During the valedictorian's speech, his friend learned something he never knew. The boy had been carrying all his books home that day because he didn't want his mother to have to clean out his locker. With tears in his eyes, he told the graduating students how he had planned to kill himself that night. All those years later, his friend learned what one small act of kindness did for someone else.

Offer to carry the books.

Be Selfishly Good

Don't do it just because *it's the right thing to do* or *the world will be a better place if we all act kindly.* Do it also for yourself. Do it for all the physical, emotional, and psychological benefits to *you.* Did you know people who regularly help others live longer? Yep, they have less stress, lower rates of depression, higher life satisfaction, and improved immune function.[7] One of the best ways to pluck yourself out of a downward emotional spiral is to help someone in need.

It is the ultimate luxury to combine passion and contribution. It's also a very clear path to happiness.
Sheryl Sandberg

Who Do I Help?

Listen, I know you don't have extra time to spend volunteering. You're too busy or exhausted to volunteer downtown this weekend. *What you need is a nap!* Yes, sometimes you need a nap. Other times though, you need to get involved in something you love *besides your immediate family and environment.* This act of helping others will bring more energy and purpose into your life.

Let me ask you this: *what topics get you fired up?* Do you want to rescue animals from puppy farms? Do you want to help children who are homeless? Do you want to help fund research for congenital heart disease? World hunger? Polluted oceans? What pulls at your heartstrings? *Not sure?* If you could snap your fingers and solve one problem in the world, what would it be?

 There is no *right* answer; just the right answer for you, right now.

If you have no idea or have so many ideas flashing through your mind that none seem better than the rest, then try this for two weeks: *I'm so grateful to know exactly what connects my passion, my talents, and my interests to benefit others.*

Another option is to go with the first idea that came to mind when you began reading this chapter. Sometimes our first idea seems silly. Or too big. Or too embarrassing. Did an idea come to mind that felt completely ridiculous or impossible? If this is the case, ask yourself, is this something you care about deeply? If so, you are on the right track. Do something this week in the direction of this idea. Call three organizations that serve this same goal or problem or population. Don't email. *Call.* Sign up to spend your time or offer your skills or resources one time in the next month. Don't wait until after the holidays, summer vacation, or your dad's knee surgery. There will always be a good reason to delay it. Do it now.

---

*If you want joy, give joy to others. If you want money,
help others to earn money. If you want compliments,
give them away freely.*
Deepak Chopra

More Than Time and Money

Yes, you can give your time or money to a cause. But, let's go deeper. Maybe you have connections that could help a given cause or an organization. A few key introductions could help tremendously. Maybe you're a fundraising wiz or a logo designer. Donate your expertise, your advice, or your talent.

Do you love to organize? Are you a great writer? What natural talents do you have that an organization could use? Maybe you love talking to people and could drum up more volunteers in the community or you're a social media maven and can create promotional content. Maybe you love to plan events. Bake pies. Audit bank statements. Maybe your aunt has an amazing backyard you could offer for a fundraising party. *Should I go on?*

Remember, there is *something* you shine at which others don't want to do, don't know how to do, or cannot afford to do. What can you offer that is unique to you?

---

*We make a living by what we get, but we make a life
by what we give.*
Winston Churchill

MINI-HOMEWORK ASSIGNMENT: (4 minutes)

1. What three talents do you have to give?
2. What causes are most important to you?
3. What ONE thing will you do this week to RADIATE yourself outward?

Give a man a fish and he has fish for the day;
teach him how to fish and you can get rid of him
for the entire weekend.
Anonymous

PART IV
BECOME EVEN BETTER

Chapter Twelve

MASTER YOUR MIND

---

*For what you see and hear depends a good deal on
where you are standing: It also depends on
what sort of person you are.*
The Magician's Nephew by C.S. Lewis

've already mentioned my bossy nature as a child. Well, I also apparently had little self-control; not a nice combination. Most of my elementary school report cards concluded, *Amber is a smart child, if only she could have a little more self-control.* By the time I made it to college, I had taken that advice to heart.

Ok, you want self-control? I'll give you self-control! I planned out each day into 15-minute slots. *Everything* I did was scheduled, organized, and checked off the appropriate list. Unfortunately, along with my super-controlled life, I lost access to my creativity and my intuition. I relied solely on the logical, organized side of my brain. If you're connected to your intuition, your creativity, and your emotions, meditation may come easily to you. It may be an extension of what you already do naturally.

But, if you're like me and have endless *iShould* chatter in your mind, *meditation is gonna rock your world.* Meditation and visualization practices quiet the mental chaos. These tools can lead to more calm, more focus, and more balance in your life.

Kinda like when you have to shut your computer down. Sometimes when it goes crazy, you just shut it down and when you turn it on, it's okay again. That's what meditation is for me.
Ellen DeGeneres

Did you know Google has a multi-million-dollar mindfulness center that houses a giant meditation room? Google isn't the only company focused on helping its employees tune-in. Nope. Twitter, Asana, Starbucks, and Aetna are just a few of the others promoting meditation to improve employee health, happiness, and work efficiency. Even the U.S. Navy SEALS has a *Mind Gym* complete with sensory deprivation tanks and brainwave training.

Did you know Clint Eastwood meditates?

Your Chemical Brain on Meditation

Remember our friend cortisol? Well, folks who meditate can reduce their cortisol levels by up to 50%.[8] Meditation will also boost your DHEA hormone levels. *Why is this a good thing?* Because it's linked to your true physiological age.[9] In other words, the more DHEA you have, the longer you have left on this planet. *Want more?* Ok, GABA is the brain chemical linked to feeling calm. Meditating even once increases the amount of GABA in your brain.[10]

Remember how you like to sleep and feel rested? Well, meditating also increases the amount of melatonin your brain makes. Melatonin strengthens your immune system. Remember the last time you were sick, but couldn't stop to rest because the world kept spinning? *Let's keep you healthy.*

Your Electrical Brain on Meditation

If you're just getting started with meditation and you're feeling uncomfortable or skeptical, guess what? You already know how to do it. *Do you ever zone out while you're going for a run? Have you come up with a brilliant idea while you're in the shower or daydreaming during a boring meeting?* In those moments, your brain on an EEG looks like it's meditating.

Think of your brain like a sorority. You've got your betas, alphas, thetas, and deltas. Each sorority house has its own unique characteristics. Only, instead of a college party house, it's a type of brain wave. Each *wave* is the result of the tiny electrical impulses released every time your brain cells communicate with each other. There are a few different types and each one depends on your state of mental alertness.

Beta waves are most common when you're awake and alert, like when you're in a conversation at work or in school. **Alpha** waves are most common when you're awake but not actively thinking or working. You're still aware of your surroundings. You feel calmer and better able to absorb, learn, and retain new information.

Theta waves are most common when you're asleep. Your inner mind has more of your attention than the outside world. These waves are linked to learning, memory, intuition, and creativity. **Delta** waves are more elusive and appear in times of deep meditation and deep, dreamless sleep. Physical healing and recovery are thought to take place in this frequency.

During meditation, your brain enters an *alpha state.* Sometimes, even a *theta state.* The more you practice, the quicker you enter alpha and the more benefits you'll reap. *Oh, the benefits. Let's talk about those!*

The Benefits of Meditation: Emotional, Mental, and Psychological

- ✓ You may feel calmer
- ✓ You may feel more patient
- ✓ You may feel more understanding of others
- ✓ You may feel more accepting of yourself
- ✓ You may feel more grateful
- ✓ You may feel less frantic and frazzled
- ✓ You may notice improvements in memory
- ✓ You may experience an increase in creativity
- ✓ You may feel happier
- ✓ You may feel more energetic

The Benefits of Meditation: Physical

- ✓ You may experience more restorative sleep
- ✓ You may experience lower blood pressure
- ✓ You may feel a reduction in chronic pain
- ✓ You may experience fewer symptoms of anxiety and depression
- ✓ You may develop a more efficient metabolism

Did you know Katy Perry meditates?

Types of Meditation

There are many different types of meditations. There are books and classes and workshops galore if you'd like to delve deeper into the meditation world. I will focus on the basic techniques so you can use meditation to improve your brain, body, and emotional states. Then, not only can you create the life you want, but you can be clear and calm enough to truly enjoy it.

Before I go further, I want to be clear on what meditation is *not*. Sukey and Elizabeth Novogratz sum it up nicely in their book, *Just Sit*. According to these ladies, meditation is not stopping your thoughts completely, a spiritual bliss-out, achieving absolute stillness, checking out of your brain, or a happy pill.

Guided Meditations

If you love technology and regularly use apps, check out HeadSpace, Insight Timer, Calm, or Omvana. These offer fantastic guided meditations that can be as short or as long as you'd like. All you need is a quiet space and the decision to prioritize meditating over 10 minutes of sleep, work, or cleaning.

Did you know George Lucas meditates?
(Yoda is rumored to be based on Transcendental
Meditation founder Maharishi Mahesh Yogi!)

Breathing Meditations

Slow, deep breathing is the simplest way to slow down your brainwaves. That's why most meditations begin with focusing in on your breath, slowing it down, and deepening it. Try sitting still with your eyes closed while you count backwards from 30 and just breathe.

If tech is more of a hindrance than a help to you, use a breathing meditation. You can look them up online or try this: count slowly as you inhale, then again as you exhale. Try to remain focused on your breath or your heartbeat. Get in a comfy but not 'fall-asleep' position and find a quiet space, with as few distractions as possible. Then, close your eyes and just breathe.

When thoughts about people or situations bubble up into your mind, imagine popping them with a pin, and then refocus on your breathing. I like to imagine I'm on a raft in a pool, and when I 'bump' into a thought, I gently push myself back into the center of the pool. Slowly, as time goes on, the pool becomes larger, and you don't hit the edges quite as often.

In my control freak brain, I even tried to *control* my meditation practice. I would see how long I could stretch out my inhales and exhales. I pushed myself further and slower with every breath. *Twenty-four seconds. Yes!*

Did you know Sir Paul McCartney meditates?

I recently learned, from Harvard Ph.D. meditation instructor, Dustin DiPerna, you're not supposed to try to control your breathing. Just notice it. Dr. DiPerna recommended I instead notice the feeling of my hands on my legs. *Booooring, yes, but that's kind of the point.* He said, through practice continually drawing my attention back to my hands each time it wanders off, I'll be better able to keep my mind focused in all areas of my life, not only during meditation. *This is a tough one for me.*

When there's a particularly toxic thought looping in my mind, like something bad might happen to one of my children or I'm worrying about how someone might react to an email I just sent out, I imagine my brain as a large cement-domed room. In my hand, I have a big hose. Sometimes, I need a broom too. I imagine spraying down the entire room and then sweeping the floor as well. I focus on the water and the walls and the floor. This helps me tremendously, even though I *hate* cleaning.

Meditation trains your brain to more readily tap into a state of focus, clarity, and calm during the 16 hours a day when you're awake and alert. It is not the experience *during* a meditation that keeps meditators practicing for years, it's all the benefits you see during the hours spent not meditating that keeps 'em coming back for more.

"I was doing a TV series in which I was the star of the show, the executive producer of the show, the head writer, in charge of casting and editing, for 24 episodes on network television... So I meditated every day. And that's how I survived the nine years."
Jerry Seinfeld

Tom Bilyeu, founder and CEO of Quest Nutrition, practices the classic "box breathing." This is when you use the same counts for your inhale, hold at the 'top' of your breath, exhale, then hold at the 'bottom' of your breath. Like a box, get it!? Don't hold so long you turn blue or are uncomfortable. If you don't like holding at the top or bottom... *then, don't do it!*

Intermediate Meditation: Zone In

Researchers on meditation and scientists studying brainwaves have found experiencing emotions like gratitude and forgiveness during your meditations can lead to higher levels of meditative states. These 'higher levels' appear to correspond to physical, psychological, and emotional changes in the meditators. So, meditating in a grumpy mood is far less impactful. Try a quick gratitude practice at the start of your meditation, and you'll dramatically increase its benefits.

Did you know Martin Scorsese meditates?

When to Meditate?

Meditate whenever and wherever you're most likely to do it. Seriously, it's that simple. As soon as you see the benefits, finding the time becomes much easier. Ideally, do it first thing in the morning and last thing before sleeping at night. Many experts now recommend meditating after some exercise. In my life, I find sitting up in bed, before I'm fully awake (or anyone else is awake in my house) is the best and quietest time for me to do it. Bottom line; **Do what works for you.**

Some Options:

- In bed before everyone else wakes up in the morning, or after everyone else goes to sleep at night.
- In the shower. *Lock the door.*
- In the car, a few blocks away from home. Just pull over and park your car, then close your eyes and breathe. Make sure your car has no children in it or groceries that need to be put away. *Actually, the milk can wait ten minutes. Go for it.*
- If you exercise, you can even do a mediation while running, swimming, walking, etc.

Dan Harris, author of *Meditation for Fidgety Skeptics*, gives great advice: *if you get distracted and forget where you are, start over from where you got lost, always with the sense of humor about your tragic gnat-like attention span.* Kintsugi comes into play here. Wasting time and energy judging yourself about how you're meditating is completely counter productive. Give yourself a break. Be kind to yourself.

Did you know Arianna Huffington meditates?

KEY MEDITATION TAKEAWAYS

1. **Don't beat yourself up.** I don't say this because I want you to be *kind* to yourself. Nope. I say it because you're more likely to quit if you set your expectations too high.

2. **Remember, it will get easier.** I'm totally addicted to meditating. The benefits I've seen in my life outweigh the time it takes. Now that I enjoy it, it's much easier to make the space in my day for that added ten minutes before bed and ten minutes in the morning.

3. *You* **know** *you.* Only you know what will work best for you. Set yourself up for success by choosing the best type of meditation, time of day, and location that appeals most to you.

If I had to live my life again,
I'd make the same mistakes, only sooner.
Tallulah Bankhead

Chapter Thirteen

CREATE YOUR FUTURE

Well, maybe it started that way. As a dream, but doesn't everything? Those buildings. These lights. This whole city. Somebody had to dream about it first, and maybe that is what I did. I dreamed about coming here, but then I did it.
James and the Giant Peach by Roald Dahl

Imagine if 30 years ago, someone described a hand-held portable screen that allowed you to communicate instantaneously with anyone, anywhere in the world. What if they told you this little device could hold thousands of pictures and movies, act as a calculator, a compass, and access the answer to almost any question imaginable in mere seconds. *Would you have believed them?*

A man named Guglielmo Marconi was ahead of his time, and nobody believed him either. In fact, he was almost institutionalized when he shared his dream of sending invisible data across miles and miles of thin air. His friends thought he'd lost his mind. *He's the guy who invented radio communication.* My point is this: just because we don't understand how something works doesn't mean it's not an incredibly valuable tool. It's possible a few decades from now, there'll be 50 million people using tools that sound unbelievable today.

I believe visualization is one of these tools.

You learned how stress and anxiety affect your memory, mood, physical health, and quality of sleep. You learned how to smash your iShould devices, uncover your Baloney Beliefs, and identify what is most important to you. You learned how to better manage your cortisol and adrenaline levels by breathing, forgiving, and letting it be. You learned how meditation affects your brain, your body, and your emotions. Now, you'll take that calm, cool, focused brain and direct it outward.

Visualization is the practice of using positive thoughts and emotions to elicit chemical states and brainwave patterns to increase your focus, creativity, and problem-solving skills. Athletes today regularly envision themselves making the shot, clearing the hurdles, or completing the perfect dive. These athletes know visualizing their goal significantly increases their odds of doing it for real. Al Oerter, a four-time Olympic discus champion and tennis phenomenon Billie Jean King were two of the first to use visualization techniques in the 1960s. Through visualization, you will use your mind and your intentions to draw what you want into your life.

First, let's start simple.

Intention Bubbles

Using Intention Bubbles can help focus your brain on what you want in your life. Intention Bubbles help calm my Neanderthal brain and distract me from anxious thought spirals. My first experience was in 2011 after I read the 1937 book *Think and Grow Rich* by Napoleon Hill. I felt inspired to create a daily I.B. with some precise goals. Before I tell you the goals, however, I want you to know I was hesitant to include this story. The amount of money is so large; I thought it might appear too good to be true. But, it happened, and it blew my mind. *So, here it goes.*

Four times a day I said, *I'm so grateful we are earning an extra $50,000 each month. I am so grateful I weigh 125 pounds. I am so grateful my kids are happy and healthy.*

After three months, the phone rang. A powerhouse fragrance company wanted to license one of my husband's photos. This was unusual for his line of work. Most of his photos are owned by the movie studios who hire him. But, for this one photoshoot of a famous teen idol, he happened to retain ownership of the pictures.

Please send us an invoice for $50,000, they requested. Oh, and they also wanted to use the photo on a special holiday line of perfumes. *Please send us a second invoice for $50,000.* Then, they said they'd used his photo for the previous year's campaign, but never paid. *So, please send us a third invoice for $50,000.* Three months. Three invoices for $50,000. I'm not saying this will happen to you. But, this experience proved to me thoughts can be more powerful than I ever imagined.

Now, I do it differently. I've learned to focus my Intention Bubbles on my REAL, deep down goals. You could have an I.B. for attracting $100,000. Then, a tornado hits your house and you receive $100,000 from your insurance company. *Yeah, that's not quite what you intended.*

My next money-related I.B. became, *I'm so grateful I have financial security.* Then, after a few years feeling financially secure, I modified it yet again. Now my I.B. is, *I'm so grateful I have complete financial freedom.* Obviously, these terms can mean different things to different people. You have to decide what it means for *you.* For me, *financial freedom* means I have enough money to achieve my Top Five goals: Family, Education, Travel, Health, and Writing.

It looks like this:

Family: I want to have the financial freedom to spend as much time as I'd like with my husband and children.

Education: I want to have the financial freedom to pay for classes, buy lots of books, and pay for museums while we travel.

Note: This doesn't necessarily mean money. Before leaving on our current adventure, I purchased a family membership at the Bay Area Discovery Museum in San Francisco. They have a reciprocal membership program with almost every science museum and children's museum across the country. This savings adds up. We average one museum a week. Six tickets, with an average ticket price of $15 per person, is $90 a week. After 64 weeks on the road, we'll save $5,760.00 in museum entrance fees alone!

Travel: We want to have the financial freedom to purchase the flights, car rentals, and house rentals required for this touring year.

Note: This means listening to my Monkey Gut and taking action when a good idea pops up: joining airline rewards programs, a Delta American Express card that pays luggage fees, and Marriott points for free breakfasts!

Health: I want to have the financial freedom to purchase healthy, organic food, and attend dance classes.

Note: Two months ago, eight new parents and their children joined the tour. Of the new mothers, three of them are professional dance teachers. *Amazing, right?* Two of them offer classes now as we go city to city on this tour. I took a class yesterday and I'm so grateful!

Writing: *I want to have the financial freedom to attend a writing workshop somewhere incredible.*

You can create Intention Bubbles for any part of your life. For instance, my little motto about this trip is, *I'm so grateful this tour is a fun, easy, educational, family adventure.* I added *fun* and *easy* a few months after we began. This I.B. helps me remember I'm not just here to survive this experience. I'm not here only to manage the flights and car rentals and make sure everyone else enjoys themselves. No, I want it to be *fun for me.* I also want it to be *easy.*

Intention Bubbles: Keep 'em Positive

Make sure your I.B. is positive. Say, *I easily arrive on time wherever I go,* instead of *I'm not going to be late anymore!* An Intention Bubble that says what you DON'T want doesn't work. You see, your brain notices nouns and verbs much more than adverbs. So 'never,' 'not,' and 'don't' get canceled out. Your Neanderthal brain absorbs the nouns and verbs. It's more positive to tell yourself *I'm not smart, kind or fun* than to say *I'm not dumb, mean or boring.* Your Neanderthal brain picks up the important words. So, keep it positive.

The Ho'oponopono

If you find yourself so distracted you don't want to make up your own, use this one: Ho'oponopono. Entrepreneur and author Joe Vitale describes a very simple technique he learned from psychologist Ihaleakala Hew Len, PhD. The Ho'oponopono is easy because it never changes. You repeat these four phrases: *I love you. I'm sorry. Please forgive me. Thank you.* I've found this helps me a lot when I cannot calm down my hamster brain enough to focus. You can say it to yourself, to whatever higher power you believe in, or to your cat. It doesn't matter. *It's all good.*

I love you. I'm sorry. Please forgive me. Thank you.

Oh GOODIE

The GOODIE Practice is my supercharged method of visualization. After reading a host of books on the subject, I noticed the same six components cropping up again and again. Writers, philosophers, and CEO's who use visualization share similar practices, despite very different jobs, backgrounds, and countries of origin. When I incorporated those six ideas into my practice, I noticed a marked improvement in my life. In order to help me remember the major elements, I came up with the acronym GOODIE: **G**ratitude, **O**utcome, **O**thers, **D**etails, **I**nspiration, and **E**motions.

Gratitude

Before bringing something better into your life, you must feel grateful for your current life. I know this can be hard, especially when you're unhappy. But, visualizing works so much better when you can focus on what you appreciate in your life *now*. This is similar to *facing forward*. If you feel upset and unhappy with your life, you're focusing on the current negatives. Let's switch that around. Think of three things you're thankful for in your current life. They don't have to be big things. You have great skin. Your kids are healthy. Your favorite restaurant is right down the street. Now, from a place of contentment and gratitude, your visualizing will be far more effective.

Feel the Gratitude.

Be thankful for what you have; you'll end up having more.
If you concentrate on what you don't have, you will never,
ever have enough.
Oprah Winfrey

Outcome

Envision the outcome or the end goal you want. Practice feeling grateful for whatever you envision, **as if you already have it.** *Wow, I'm so thankful to live in this beautiful home in a city I love, surrounded by great neighbors.* Note: make sure you're envisioning the outcome you truly want. For instance, *I envision being VP of Sales in my company.* What does becoming the Vice President of Sales *mean* to you? *I will get a raise and have flexible hours. When I get a raise and have more flexible hours, then I can have more free time and money to do what I want. If I have more time, money, and flexibility, then I want to travel to South America and learn to speak Spanish.* Are you sure you want to be a V.P.? Or, do you want the time and resources to travel and learn a new language? Which one is the *outcome* you truly want?

What you think is your goal may not bring you what you truly desire. What if you get that VP position, and find yourself working long hours surrounded by angry, anxious, and petty coworkers? Understanding what you *really* want is the most important step. Envision your ultimate goal. Author Vishen Lakhani suggests the best way to get to your *end goal* is to ask yourself, *Because, that would mean what?* Ask it over and over until you cannot get any clearer.

For instance: *I want a new hous*e. Because that would mean *I could stop spending all my money repairing this old house.* Because that would mean *I could save more money and time.* Because that would mean *I could invest that money and time in my jewelry business.* Because that would mean *I could quit my part-time job and spend my days making jewelry.* Because that would mean *I will be happy and fulfilled working for myself and making art.* So, ask yourself: Do you want a new house? Or, do you want to work for yourself and make jewelry all day? You may have heard people say, *let go of the 'how'.* Often, we cannot see the clearest way to get to our ultimate goal. Why limit yourself to only one path when there may be a better path not even evident to us at the time?

Envision the outcome you truly want.

Others

Remember being Selfishly Good? Let's use what you learned in the Radiate chapter to fuel your visualization practice. Include anyone who will benefit from your vision becoming a reality – the more, the merrier. Maybe your husband will feel less financial pressure. Maybe your children will see you *super*modeling your resilience and tenacity. Maybe your friends will feel inspired to follow their passions. Maybe your customers will enjoy your jewelry and feel great wearing it.

Imagine the benefits to others.

Details

To maximize the benefits of visualization, use ALL of your senses. You've gotta really sink into it. Pile on all the specifics you can muster. Get lost in the details. Make it as real as possible. This is the practice of fooling your brain. You're connecting neurons and firing up pathways.

Remember when I wanted to be on a tropical island? I was fed up with Los Angeles: the people, the traffic, and the hectic life I'd created for myself. Well, I didn't *only* wear long dresses. I also began envisioning myself sitting on a rock, looking out at a beautiful ocean, my kids playing down on the beach below. I imagined the wind in my hair. I felt the sun on my cheeks. I heard the ocean waves hitting the sand. I sipped hot coffee from a big blue porcelain mug.

Life favors the specific ask and punishes the vague wish.
Tim Ferriss

Two weeks later the phone rang. *Are you available for a job on Oahu this summer?* At first, the timing for the trip was a bit off. The job started before the kids were out of school for the summer. I kept envisioning and feeling grateful. Miraculously, we got a call they'd 'pushed' the shoot, and now we could all fly together and enjoy the entire five weeks on the island of Oahu. It was an incredible adventure!

Note: If you're rolling your eyes and ready to chuck this book out the window after reading that last paragraph, let me ask you this: *What is the harm in trying?* This technique is free, without side effects, and the worst-case scenario is you spend a few minutes each day imagining yourself doing something you love. Best-case scenario, it happens for real.

Immerse yourself in the details.

Inspiration

You cannot force or control how something will come into your life. However, you can listen, pay attention, and meditate. Remember your Monkey Gut? When the inspiration pops up, you must jump on it as quickly as you can. Take action right away. Even if it is a seemingly small action, do it. Do not wait until you have time to do it *right*.

When you feel a hint of intuition, do something. *Now.* Stop what you're doing, pull the car over, get out of line at the grocery store and make the phone call. This is not a *just write it down* type of thing. You have to make a ripple in the water. Text, call, email, rent a skywriter. *Move in a forward direction.*

Arianna Huffington, president of Huffington Post Media Group, took inspired action after finding herself in the emergency room. Her lack of self-care brought her wealth but cost her health. As a result of her experience, Arianna embarked on a mission encouraging women "stop wearing work and stress as a badge of honor." Instead of suffering alone, Arianna realized many women shared this lack of self-care and used her epiphany to inspire a Sleep Revolution.

Take inspired action.

Emotions

Adding emotion to your visualization practice is the final piece of the puzzle. Emotion amps up the effectiveness and speed of your visualization practice. How do you *feel* when you get what you want? Excited? Relaxed? Joyful? Try to sit in that positive emotion. Feel now how you will feel once you have what you want. This is why the details and the outcome are so important. When you include all the details, it's easier to bring in positive emotions.

Feel the excitement.

Don't Change Your Order

Meditation expert Emily Fletcher tells a great story about ordering dinner. Say you sit down in a restaurant and order a steak with potatoes. Then, ten minutes later you decide you'd like the salmon with broccoli instead. Five more minutes pass and you realize you're not terribly hungry. But, dessert sounds good! You call the waiter over and apologetically change your order to a banana split and some coffee. Thirty minutes after sitting down at the table, you still have no food in front of you. *Now you're irritated and starving.*

Meanwhile, the cook has been frantically preparing each of your orders. But, before she could serve each dish, you changed your mind. Visualization does not happen instantaneously.

Order what you want, be patient, and give the cook some time to make it.

In a recent Stretch Marks Retreat, one woman shared how her spiritual beliefs precluded her from attempting to manifest a specific outcome in her life. According to her religion, life proceeds according to a greater plan, and she felt uncomfortable envisioning a particular event or situation. If this perspective resonates with you, I recommend using emotions as your ultimate vision. Feelings of joy, calm, confidence, safety, and excitement can be the outcome you envision.

MINI-HOMEWORK ASSIGNMENT (6 minutes)

1. Start an Intention Bubble. Pick something simple. Try repeating it three times in the morning and three times before bed every day.
2. Start a G.O.O.D.I.E practice: **What do you want?**

   For Example: I want a new creative career that still allows me time with my family.

   Gratitude: *I'm so grateful my parents are healthy, my kids love their school, and I got to take a nice long bath last night.*

   Outcome: *I'm excited to work with great people, have flexible hours, and use my brain in a creative way.*

   Others: *My kids are happier because I'm less stressed, my husband is less worried about finances, and my dog loves that I'm home early to take him for walks.*

Details: *I can smell the coffee. I can feel the breeze on my face as I drive to the office. I can see the new work clothes I get to wear every day. I can hear the chatter in the restaurant downstairs from the office, where we have a lunch meeting. I can taste the delicious pasta with garlic sauce.*

Inspiration: Notice what happens around you. Be on alert. What thoughts or ideas pop into mind first thing in the morning? *Oh, you remember your college friend works in this field and used to live in your hometown?* Email or call her that day. *Oh, you remember a neighbor talking about a new company that sounded interesting.* Walk over to his house and ask about it. Today.

I find meditation and feeling calmer allows me to notice these little nuggets of inspiration. The quicker you act on them, the more often they pop up.

Emotion: Feel it. Try to feel all the positive emotions you will experience once this dream is a reality. Pride? Excitement? Contentment? Joy? Confidence?

The GOODIE Review

G - Feel grateful for now
O - Envision the outcome you want
O - Imagine others benefitting
D - Include the details
I - Take inspired action
E - Feel the positive emotions

---

*I always wanted to be somebody, but now I realize
I should have been more specific.*
Lily Tomlin

CONCLUSION

ongratulations! You've come so far. *Unless you skipped ahead in which case you've missed so much!* Either way, you have the rest of your life ahead of you. You're the captain of your ship. You can go anywhere. I hope you take the time to slow down and breathe. I hope you *Smash Your iShoulds* over and over until they cannot muster a single *beep*. I hope you *Listen to Your Monkey Gut* to find the inspiration, ideas, and answers you seek. I hope you *Kintsugi Yourself* so you can spend your valuable time and energy on what you want in your life instead of hiding your weaknesses and mistakes.

I also hope you share your wins with me as you continue on your journey. I'm very excited to read and learn from *you*. Please email me at stretchmarksretreat@gmail.com so I can (with your permission) include them in my next book. Yes, the *Stretch Marks* books on Parenting and Money are already underway!

Before you leave, I have one last story to share. The tremendous changes in my life all started with a tiny spark. *Often, that's how it happens.* A little spark sets off a subtle chain reaction. As the weeks and months pass, your brain rewires itself, your perspective shifts, and new opportunities come into focus. Suddenly you realize your desire for change has been heating up for quite a while and only looking back can you recall the exact moment it all began.

My spark came from a book. *Big surprise, right?* I was with my kids at the local library. The boys were stocking up on books, and I took a moment to peruse the non-fiction aisle. That's when a white book with the word 'code' caught my eye. I've always been a sucker for codes and love the idea of advanced math, though I never had the skills to take it very far (read *Fermat's Theorem* if you love math and logic but aren't particularly good at it.) I pulled *Code of the Extraordinary Mind*, by Vishen Lakhiani, off the shelf and added it to the heap of books on the checkout counter.

At the start of the book, Vishen warns his readers their relationships, careers, and entire lives could be shaken up by the words within. *Eye roll.* I might decide to get divorced, change my religion, or quit my job and move to Alaska. *Easy now. I'm quite happy in my marriage, and I don't have a job, so I think I'm safe thank you very much.*

I loved this book. It made me think about my life, my perspective on beliefs, and introduced me to the many other books I devoured in the following months. That spark lit a fuse that ignited hope and excitement about my future. *Three months later…* I decided to move all four of my kids out of traditional school, dropped the belief I would always live in Los Angeles, and opened my eyes to a world of opportunities I never before considered possible. *I'm sorry I doubted you Vishen. Your book was, in fact, the catalyst for huge and wonderful change in my life and altered the course of my family.*

My greatest dream is at least one idea in these pages lights a tiny spark, a flicker of fire that ignites in you a burning passion only quelled by the utter joy of doing and having and becoming everything imaginable in your wildest dreams.

SUMMARY:

A Review of the Juiciest Tidbits

Chapter 1: TOP FIVE

Check off the five areas that are most important to you at this particular time in your life:

☐ Spending Time with Friends
☐ Playing Music/Listening to Music
☐ Problem Solving
☐ Being In Nature
☐ Feeling a Sense of Accomplishment
☐ Spending Time with Family
☐ Exercise (Specifically: _____)
☐ Cooking
☐ Traveling
☐ Helping Others
☐ Writing
☐ Reading
☐ Inspiring Others
☐ Making Art

☐ Spending Time Alone
☐ _____
☐ _____
☐ _____

Write out your Top Five. Use the notes page in your phone, post it on your computer, or write it in bright red lipstick on your bathroom mirror.

For Example: *I want to be with my family, dance, help others, travel, and learn something new.*

Chapter 2: PURPOSE POCKETS

As you go through your day, pause for a few seconds before each *pocket*. A pocket could be a meeting at work, soccer practice with the kids, or dinner out with your dad. Immediately before each pocket, take a few seconds and decide what you want. For example: *Tonight, I want to have a delicious dinner with my family and get reconnected, with no devices and lots of smiles and laughter.* It's simple and shouldn't take a lot of thought or preparation. Go with *your Monkey Gut* on this one.

Purpose Pockets force you to make conscious choices throughout your day. These choices are then more likely to align with what is *truly* important to you. Your focus shifts from what you *do not want* in your life to what you *do want* in your life.

Benefits of Purpose Pockets
✓ Allows you to focus on the present
✓ Puts you back in the captain's seat
✓ Reminds you what is most important

How To Do It:

Choose 2-3 things you want to do, on *purpose*, during the next *pocket* of your day. You can keep a little notebook, say it aloud, or sing it in your car.

Chapter 3: TIPS FOR WOMEN

Getting More Sleep

Instead of spending 20 minutes before bed on your phone, TV, or computer, turn it off. Say three things you're thankful for, then close your eyes. *Don't even read this book!*

Just breathe and notice your thoughts. Try not to get wrapped up in them. Get ahold of a sound machine, blackout curtains, and have the kids draw a no-entry sign for your bedroom door.

Spending Time with Adult Women

In person is best. Get a neighbor to go on a quick walk with you. Make friends at the park, market, or anywhere. Believe me; those other moms are just as desperate for a social connection. These people need not become life long friends, so don't worry about being super picky.

Getting A Hug

Ask a loved one for a 7-second hug once a day. Most women need daily, physical, non-romantic touch. *And no, your 4-year-old dragging himself along the floor attached to your leg does not count!*

Hearing Words of Appreciation

The secret to this one is a bit counter intuitive but try it anyway. *Give* genuine words of appreciation. Not to just anyone. Give these words to the same folks you want to hear appreciation from most.

The key is this: you have to do it genuinely and with no expectation of return. Even if you're feeling irritated and resentful toward everyone, try to find *something* to compliment. If done genuinely and consistently, you will see magical results.

Chapter 4: KIDS TOP FOUR

Remember your Top Five from the first chapter? Well, here we go again. This time though, it's about the kids, and there are only four. Scan through these characteristics and check the four you deem MOST important:

- ☐ Kind
- ☐ Generous
- ☐ Persistent
- ☐ Patient
- ☐ Resilient
- ☐ Compassionate
- ☐ Tenacious
- ☐ Humble
- ☐ Creative
- ☐ Courageous
- ☐ Passionate
- ☐ Honest
- ☐ Independent
- ☐ Empathetic
- ☐ Confident
- ☐ Other _____
- ☐ Other _____

If you had trouble choosing, finish this sentence:

Upon graduation, your child's high school advisor says to you, *Wow! How did you raise someone so...*_____

_____

_____.

Example: creative, kind, passionate, and independent
Example: confident, honest, tenacious, and resilient
Example: adventurous, patient, curious, and trustworthy

1. Talk about your Top Four in front of your children.
2. Use your Top Four to support your discipline decisions.
3. Encourage your Top Four through praise and modeling.

NOTES ON COMPETITION

- Winning is awesome, but temporary.
- Winning doesn't reflect your value as a human.
- True fairness is each child getting what *they* need when *they* need it.

Chapter 5: NOTES ON DISCIPLINE

1. Remember, *you* own everything. *Teaching the responsibility of ownership is great. But, if they're not respecting your parental rules, then maybe they don't deserve it.*
2. Be a Supermodel. *Be an example of the traits you want to encourage.*
3. Chunk yourself. *Show them you're not perfect, and you're always trying to improve yourself.*

Chapter 6: NOTES ON TECHNOLOGY

1. Decide on technology rules based on what *you* want for *your* family.
2. Follow through on your plan. Change it when necessary.
3. Always remember, you're the boss, and you own everything.

Chapter 7: WRITE YOUR OWN EULOGY

Although we will all miss Pat dearly, we can take solace knowing he/she lived an incredible life and was one of the happiest people I've ever known. Pat spent so much of his/her time doing what he/she loved most which was_____ and _____

_____.

Pat was surrounded by those he/she loved most like _____ and _____.

Pat was incredibly happy when he/she accomplished his/her dream of _____

_____.

I will always remember Pat as _____, _____, and _____.

Once you've filled in the eulogy blanks above, you will have a good idea which traits and actions rank highest on your list. These are what you value most. So, how much of your time, energy and resources do you spend on the activities and people you listed above? How often do you act in a way that corresponds to the qualities you listed?

Right now, what percentage of your time, energy, and resources do you spend on what is most important to you?
10%   25%   50%   75%   90%

What's your goal percentage?

Chapter 8: GET YOURSELF MOVING

1. What is your most productive time of day?
2. Do you work best with a team, a partner, or alone?
3. Who can you share your goals with for support, encouragement, and accountability?

Which of the following tools laid out in this chapter appealed to you most?

- ☐ Create Your *Stop It* List
- ☐ 80/20 Analysis
- ☐ Parkinson's Law
- ☐ MicroGoals
- ☐ Gamify It
- ☐ High Performer Tricks

Chapter 9: THE BALONEY BELIEFS QUIZ

Let's try uncovering some of your *Baloney Beliefs*. Fill in the following blanks:

1. Making over _____ dollars a year will never happen for me. (40,000? 250,000? 4 Million!?)
2. Weighing _____ lbs will never be a reality for me.
3. Having a career where I can _____ is just impossible for me right now. (Work part time? Work from home? Travel more? Travel less?)
4. Having a partner who treats me like _____ is never gonna happen.

5. Spending two weeks in _____ with
   _____ doing _____
   is only a fantasy.

Chapter 10: GET BALANCED *CHEMICALLY*

Balance cortisol and reduce adrenaline levels with your body and mind by:

1. Breathing more deeply
2. Chewing gum
3. Feeding yourself
4. Moving your body
5. Learning to let it be
6. Forgiving yourself and others
7. Feeling grateful for what you already have in your life.

Chapter 11: RADIATE YOURSELF

---

1. What three talents do you have to give?
2. What causes are most important to you?
3. What ONE thing will you do this week to RADIATE yourself outward?

Chapter 12: KEY MEDITATION NOTES

Don't beat yourself up. I don't say this because I want you to be *kind* to yourself. Nope. I say it because you're more likely to quit if you set your expectations too high.

Remember, it will get easier. I'm totally addicted to meditating. The benefits I've seen in my life outweigh the time it takes. Now that I enjoy it, it's much easier to make the space in my day for that added ten minutes before bed and ten minutes in the morning.

You know *you*. Only you know what will work best for you. Set yourself up for success by choosing the best type of meditation, time of day, and location that appeals most to you.

The Benefits:

- ✓ You may feel calmer
- ✓ You may feel more patient
- ✓ You may feel more understanding of others
- ✓ You may feel more accepting of yourself
- ✓ You may feel more grateful
- ✓ You may feel less frantic and frazzled
- ✓ You may notice improvements in memory
- ✓ You may experience an increase in creativity
- ✓ You may feel happier
- ✓ You may feel more energetic
- ✓ You may experience more restorative sleep
- ✓ You may experience lower blood pressure
- ✓ You may feel a reduction in chronic pain
- ✓ You may experience fewer symptoms of anxiety and depression
- ✓ You may develop a more efficient metabolism

Chapter 13: CREATE A GOODIE VISUALIZATION

G - Feel grateful for now
O - Envision the outcome you want
O - Imagine others benefitting

D – Include the details

I - Take inspired action

E - Feel the positive emotions

Example GOODIE: *I want a new creative career that still allows me time with my family.*

Gratitude: *I'm so grateful my parents are healthy, my kids love their school, and I got to take a nice long bath last night.*

Outcome: *I'm excited to work with great people, have flexible hours, and use my brain in a creative way.*

Others: *My kids are happier because I'm less stressed, my husband is less worried about finances, and my dog loves that I'm home early to take him for walks.*

Details: *I can smell the coffee. I can feel the breeze on my face as I drive to the office. I can see the new work clothes I get to wear every day. I can hear the chatter in the restaurant downstairs from the office, where we have a lunch meeting. I can taste the delicious pasta with garlic sauce.*

Inspiration: Notice what happens around you. Be on alert. What thoughts or ideas pop into mind first thing in the morning? *Oh, you remember your college friend works in this field and used to live in your hometown?* Email or call her that day. *Oh, you remember a neighbor talking about a new company that sounded interesting.* Walk over to his house and ask about it. Today.

Emotion: Feel it. Try to feel all the positive emotions you will experience once this dream is a reality. Pride? Excitement? Contentment? Joy? Confidence?

ABOUT THE AUTHOR

Amber Trueblood currently uses her eight years of graduate school and a Marriage and Family Therapy License *(unless she forgot to pay the membership fees this year, which is entirely possible)* to wrangle, enlighten, coerce, and inspire her four sons, write, and hosts Stretch Marks Retreats across the U.S.

She currently lives with her family in various hotels, short-term rental houses, and nowhere in particular, with all her worldly belongings in storage in Los Angeles, California.

Amber's tribe consists of her photographer husband, Jaimie, and their 6-, 8-, 9- and 11-year-old sons. *Yes, all sons.* In addition to writing and copyrighting an original song, Amber has painted and sold over $20,000 of original artwork, completed two sprint triathlons, and auditioned for America's Got Talent *(she hopes nobody uncovers a video)*.

Amber felt compelled to write this book to help parents find the tools they need to slow down, breathe more deeply, and create more joy in their lives.

Stretch Marks is her debut book.

If you would like to know more, you can keep up with her family's shenanigans on www.thetruebloodzone.com.

BOOK RECOMMENDATIONS

I am a bibliophile: *a person who collects or has a great love of books.* Five minutes after meeting me, it's likely I'll recommend a book. I suggest books to Lyft drivers. I share titles with flight attendants. I mention random books to strangers in line at the market.

So, while most books do not include a Book Recommendations page, I cannot resist sharing my absolute favorites with you! I'll break them down by area, so you can select what might interest you most. *I'm so excited!*

The ASK Mindset: Finding What You Want
- *The Element* by Ken Robinson, PhD
- *Making Your Dreams Come True* by Marcia Wieder

The MOVE Mindset: How to Make it Happen
- *Tools of Titans* by Tim Ferriss (This one is a monster. But, well worth it. Put it in your bathroom and read one page a day for the next three years.)
- *The ONE Thing* by Gary Keller

The BELIEVE Mindset: Uncover Baloney Beliefs
- *Code of the Extraordinary Mind* by Vishen Lakhiani
- *Stealing Fire* by Steven Kotler and Jamie Wheal

The ELEVATE Mindset: Improving Your Body and Mind
- *Game Changers* by Dave Asprey
- *The Superhuman Mind* by Berit Brogaard and Kristian Marlow

The RADIATE Mindset:
- *Seven Spiritual Laws of Success* by Deepak Chopra
- *Cracking the Millionaire Code* by Mark Victor Hansen and Robert G. Allen (Don't let the title fool you, this one is about *far more* than money.)

Master Your Mind
- *Meditation for Fidgety Skeptics* by Dan Harris
- *Just Sit* by Sukey Novogratz and Elizabeth Novogratz

Create Your Future
- *Into the Magic Shop* by James R. Doty, M.D.
- *The Law of Attraction* by Esther and Jerry Hicks

Parenting
- *Siblings Without Rivalry* by Adele Faber and Elaine Mazlish (If you have one, two, six or zero children, you'll enjoy this book. It's brilliant, quick, easy, and entertaining to read.)
- *The Boy Crisis* by Warren Farrell, Ph.D. and John Gray, Ph.D.

Relationships
- *Beyond Mars and Venus* by John Gray

Writing
- *On Writing* by Stephen King
- *Still Writing* by Dani Shapiro

Business

- *Delivering Happiness* by Tony Hsieh (CEO of Zappos)
- *It's Not Rocket Science* by Mary Spio (Deep Space Engineer, CEO of CEEK VR)

Light and Inspiring

- *Living with a Seal* by Jesse Itzler
- *The Rosie Project* by Graeme Simsion
- *How to be Miserable* by Randy J. Paterson, Ph.D.

If any two books could be mandatory reading for every human on the planet, I would choose these two books. *Don't let their titles fool you; they were both written a very long time ago.*

- *How to Win Friends and Influence People* by Dale Carnegie
- *Think and Grow Rich* by Napoleon Hill

If everyone read the last two on my list, our world would focus less on differences and blaming others, and focus more on creative solutions, compassion, and love. Now that's a world I'll happily leave for future generations.

CALL TO ACTION

Want more?

Check out www.thetruebloodzone.com for the latest videos, tips, and articles.

The Stretch Marks Retreat

Want to feel calm, get connected, and create the next phase of your life at a *Stretch Marks Retreat?* This wonderful getaway follows The A.M.B.E.R. Mindsets to allow you the time and space to rest, think, and get inspired in a beautiful, relaxing resort setting. Email me at stretchmarksretreat@gmail.com for an application.

Did you enjoy this book?

If you found this book entertaining, enlightening, or inspiring, please email me, share your thoughts via your favorite online book retailer, *or call Oprah's people to let them know.* You can also nominate it for your next book club read, buy a copy for your sister-in-law, or give it away at baby showers.

Thank you so much for taking the time to read this book. See you next time!

Warmly,
Amber Trueblood

Endnotes

1 Gilkes, Madeline (2017, December 18) *Cortisol Production and Use by the Body* retrieved on May 6, 2018 from https://www.ausmed.com/articles/cortisol-production-use-body/

2 Bailey, Gary (February 2017) *How Adrenaline Affects Your Body retrieved* on June 10, 2018 from http://successunder-pressure.com/2018/01/24/adrenaline-affects-body/

3 Dennis, Rebecca (March 2017) *The Health Benefits of Deep Breathing: 9 Ways it Supercharges Your Body and Mind* re-trieved on May 10, 2018 from https://www.consciouslife-stylemag.com/benefits-of-breathing-deeply/

4 Scholey, Andrew et.al. Chewing gum alleviates negative mood and reduces cortisol during acute laboratory psycho-logical stress, Journal of Physiology and Behavior, 2009, June 22; 97(3-4):304-12 retrieved on May 6, 2018 from https://www.ncbi.nlm.nih.gov/pubmed/19268676

5 *https://www.apa.org/news/press/releases/2017/11/lowest-point. aspx November 1, 2017* APA *Stress in America*™ Survey: US at 'Lowest Point We Can Remember;' Future of Nation Most Commonly Reported Source of Stress

6 https://www.ncbi.nlm.nih.gov/pubmed/25736389 J Health Psychol. 2016 Oct;21(10):2207-17. doi: 10.1177/1359105315572455. Epub 2015 Mar 2. The im-

pact of a brief gratitude intervention on subjective well-being, biology and sleep. Jackowska M[1], Brown J[2], Ronaldson A[2], Steptoe A[2].

7   Mental Floss, The 7 Scientific Benefits of Helping Others retrieved on June 10, 2018 from http://mentalfloss.com/article/71964/7-scientific-benefits-helping-others

8   J Med Assoc Thai. 2013 Jan;96 Suppl 1:S90-5. Effects of mindfulness meditation on serum cortisol of medical students. Turakitwanakan W[1], Mekseepralard C, Busarakumtragul P. https://www.ncbi.nlm.nih.gov/pubmed/23724462

9   Project Meditation, *Bad News for Your Health and Well-Being* retrieved on May 18, 2018 from https://www.project-meditation.org/bad-news-for-your-health-and-your-well-being/

10 Streeter, Chris et.al. *Journal of Alternative and Complementary Medicine*, 2010 Nov; 16(11):1145-1152. Effects of Yoga Verses Walking on Mood, Anxiety, and Brain GABA Levels: A Randomized Controlled MRS Study. https://www.ncbi.nlm.nih.gov/pmc/articles/PMC3111147/

CPSIA information can be obtained
at www.ICGtesting.com
Printed in the USA
BVHW030353260220
573364BV00004B/11